"Mr. Speaker, it is for this generation, for this Parliament, to give them and all of us a common flag; a Canadian flag which, while bringing together but rising above the landmarks and milestones of the past, will say proudly to the world and to the future: 'I stand for Canada.'"

LESTER BOWLES PEARSON, June 15, 1964

A Flag for

Canada

Rick Archbold

STANTON ATKINS & DOSIL PUBLISHERS

Vancouver

CONTENTS

This rare lapel pin dating from before the First World War proves that as early as the first decade of the twentieth century, the maple leaf helped send the message "Buy Canadian."

CHAPTER ONE

Identity crisis

AS LESTER B. "MIKE" PEARSON relaxed in the prime ministerial seat of the government jet taking him to Winnipeg on the afternoon of Saturday, May 16, 1964, he leafed casually through back issues of *The Legionary*, the magazine of the Royal Canadian Legion. Skimming article after article condemning his flag policy, he must have felt some anxiety about the speech he would be giving Sunday evening to the Legion's twentieth Dominion Convention. From the moment Mike Pearson promised Canadians a flag of their own, the Legion had been among his loudest critics, second only to Tory leader John Diefenbaker, whom he'd recently deposed as prime minister. A decisive majority of the Legion's quarter-million members – all of them veterans of Canada's armed forces – seemed to stand behind the cover of their magazine, which for months had borne a picture of the Canadian Red Ensign with the caption, "This Is Canada's Flag: Keep It Flying."

Pearson knew that if his speech went well – if his audience listened with respect – then he would be commended for his courage in facing his critics and speaking his mind. But if the old warriors shouted

him down, if he looked weak or vacillating, he would be pilloried and his cause damaged. Yet according to John Matheson, the Liberal MP for Leeds who was Pearson's parliamentary secretary and his right-hand man on the flag issue, "Nothing appeared to bother him. When he stepped off the plane in Winnipeg it was obvious he felt at home and relaxed. He might as well have been with intimate old comrades from Gallipoli or the Royal Flying Corps."

Did the prime minister even notice as he was being driven to his hotel that from every building and flagpole and from every light standard along Portage Avenue there flapped a Red Ensign or a Union Jack? Did he remember that Winnipeg was the birthplace of the Royal Canadian Legion? Did he wonder if he'd made a dreadful mistake? Wisely, Matheson had persuaded Pearson to bring along his medals, something he'd been reluctant to do. He was, after all, one of them, a veteran of the First World War. And as one of them, he surely knew how hard-minded they would be when it came to matters of patriotic principle.

Sunday evening, nearly two thousand delegates and their wives crowded into

Canada's 1964 Flag Debate mesmerized the country and provoked passionate argument on both sides of the issue. On June 1, 1964, as the parliamentary struggle was about to begin, supporters of the Canadian Red Ensign gathered on Parliament Hill to demonstrate. The RCMP was also out in force – to keep the pro-ensign crowd away from those demonstrating for Pearson's new, three-maple-leaf flag.

Lester Pearson arrives at the podium before his Winnipeg speech, escorted by a group of legionnaires. The Capitol Theatre was packed tight with members and their wives, many of them wearing Red Ensign pins in protest against the prime minister's flag policy.

Winnipeg's Capitol Theatre as the Legion president, Judge Clare C. Sparling, who had publicly called for a national plebiscite on the flag question, introduced the prime minister. The podium was lit by garish television lights being used by the CBC crew that all but blinded the guest speaker. Perhaps the lights saved Pearson from contemplating the Red Ensigns pinned to many a legionnaire's lapel, a sea of silent protest. Polite applause followed the introduction. Then Pearson began.

Canada's fourteenth prime minister was a great orator, but a commanding presence he was not. His predilection for bow ties made him look more like the university professor and Ottawa mandarin he had been than the national leader he now was. His slight lisp tended to undercut his attempts at sounding dignified and made him too easy to parody. His public diffidence, his self-deprecating manner seldom moved or inspired.

First Pearson talked about hospital care for veterans, a topic near to the hearts of his audience. The legionnaires listened quietly and applauded politely. Then he turned to his main subject.

"Members of the Legion are aware of my Government's commitment, made by our party some years ago, to ask Parliament to decide on a distinctive Canadian flag within a certain period of time. I, too, am very much aware of your Legion executive's current attitude towards that Government policy." The audience stirred and muttered. "This mutual awareness of our attitudes, I believe, precludes any possibility that I should appear before you tonight and attempt to dodge the flag issue. After all, you are men who know what it means to go into battle! So I intend to talk briefly, but frankly, about this issue: To put my own feelings, my beliefs, my judgment squarely and honestly before you. You would expect me to do this and I believe it is my duty also. I expect dissent. I also respect it."

The prime minister seemed to be in good form, speaking well and forcefully. But he had yet to challenge his listeners. "Mr. Chairman, when I went overseas in 1915 I had as comrades in my section men whose names were Cameron, Kimura, English, Bleidenstein, O'Shaughnessy, De Chapin. We didn't fall in, or fall out, as Irish Canadians, French Canadians, Japanese

> "It's not a question of logic. It's a question of emotion. And a flag is an emotional thing."
>
> DONALD THOMPSON, national secretary of the Royal Canadian Legion, May 18, 1964

Canadians, Dutch Canadians. We wore the same uniform with the same maple leaf badge" – at the words "maple leaf" a few boos came back from the audience – "and we were proud to be known as Canadians, to serve as Canadians and to die, if that had to be, as Canadians. I wish our country had more of that spirit today, of unity, 'togetherness,' and resolve; the spirit that was shown by Canadians in time of war when the survival of our country was at stake. Well, the survival of our country as a united and strong federal state is at stake today."

So far, the audience seemed willing to give him a hearing, and the prime minister seemed to be settling into his speech. Maybe this was not going to be as tough as everyone had predicted.

"What we need is a patriotism that will put Canada ahead of its parts," Pearson continued, warming up for the main punch of his argument. "Our ties to the mother country do not now include any trace of political subordination." He was conveniently forgetting that the Canadian constitution was still an act of the British parliament. "They are ties of affection, of tradition and respect. As a Canadian,

I don't want them destroyed or weakened. But they have changed, and the symbols of Canada have changed with them. This is an inevitable process. In World War I, the flag that flew for Canadian soldiers overseas was the Union Jack." Pearson, who had not served in France, believed this to be true; many veterans in his audience who had fought in the trenches remembered seeing the Red Ensign used, if unofficially, by the soldiers at the front. "In World War II, in January 1944, the Red Ensign came officially on the scene…"

At the words "Red Ensign" loud cheering erupted in the hall, forcing the prime minister to pause. A group of troublemakers in the audience raised a Red Ensign on a pole and waved it above the crowd. A large number of legionnaires stood up and roared in approval. As the cheers persisted, Judge Sparling attempted to quiet the ruckus by brandishing his gavel. When the shouting subsided, he admonished the assembly: "I thought you were all ladies and gentlemen. This is an honoured guest invited here." As the protesters sat back down one of them yelled, "No, throw him out!"

The prime minister soldiered on, pointing out that the Legion's own badge, adopted after much debate, featured a single maple leaf. "I believe that today a flag designed around the maple leaf will symbolize – will be a true reflection of – the new Canada." Loud boos filled the hall. One veteran shouted out, "We don't want it, we've got a flag!" Another voice called out, "Where is your flag?" And another: "Put it to the people!"

Pearson tried valiantly to stay with his text and on his message. "Would such a change mean disrespect for the Union Jack?" "Yes!" the crowd roared back, drowning the prime minister's answer. He plowed forward, vowing not to abandon the Union Jack but arguing that it should become "a symbol of our membership in the Commonwealth of Nations and of our loyalty to the Crown."

The audience had now reached a pitch of rowdiness that made it difficult for the prime minister to be heard. "You're selling us out to the pea-soupers," someone shouted. Came another: "God save Diefenbaker." And another: "Keep the Red Ensign." And yet another: "Go home!"

Duncan Macpherson's cartoon in the *Toronto Star* brilliantly satirized Pearson's confrontation with the Legion. The prime minister emerged from the Winnipeg trenches looking both courageous and visionary.

It had become impossible for Pearson to continue. Judge Sparling attempted to gavel the hall into relative quiet. "It's all right, Mr. Chairman," Pearson retorted. "This is a veterans' meeting." The comment prompted laughter and some applause that seemed to shift the mood somewhat in the prime minister's favour. "I remember Harry Truman saying, 'If you can't stand the heat, get out of the kitchen.'" More laughter and clapping. Mike had not been rattled. He could take the heat.

Although the heckling continued during the rest of the speech, much of the crowd listened, and the booing came less frequently. Undeniably Pearson was making his case and making it well. And he clearly meant what he said.

"I believe most sincerely that it is now time for Canadians to unfurl a flag that is truly distinctive and truly national in character; as Canadian as the maple leaf which should be its dominant design, a flag easily identifiable as Canada's; a flag which cannot be mistaken for the emblem of any other country; a flag of the future which honours also the past; Canada's own and only Canada's."

This time the boos and catcalls came mixed with applause. Perhaps the legionnaires were not unanimous in their attachment to the Canadian Red Ensign. Next, Pearson quoted the Tory premier of Nova Scotia, Robert Stanfield, who would one day face him across the Commons aisle as leader of the opposition. "Surely the Canadian thing for us to do is to find symbols which are mutually acceptable. Let us emphasize what we have in common."

The prime minister now brought his speech to an idealistic conclusion: "I want to add, ladies and gentlemen, that while I am concerned about this whole question of national symbols, national anthem, national flag, and all they mean to our country, I am even more concerned with making Canada the kind of country – with freedom, economic security, social justice, and opportunity for all – over which we will be proud to have our flag fly."

A few more words to wind things down and then Mike Pearson stepped away from the microphone. Many in the crowd – perhaps half of them – stood to applaud. Quite a few sat grimly on their hands. To another ovation, Pearson accepted an

honorary life membership in the Legion. "It has been a very interesting evening," he said, prompting much laughter.

The following day, Pearson's Winnipeg speech was condemned as provocative and praised as courageous. In the days that followed, the public response in the letters that poured into his Parliament Hill office was overwhelmingly supportive. It appeared that the prime minister's gamble had paid off. He had faced his toughest audience and held firm. But could he maintain that momentum through what promised to be one of the most divisive debates in House of Commons history?

IT IS HARD TO RECALL NOW, more than forty years later, just how big a deal the flag question was: the passions it aroused; the divisions it deepened; the crisis in Confederation it amplified. But Canada was a very different country in 1964 – a former colony that had not quite finished growing up to adult nationhood. It was clearly a country on the move – its population swelled by postwar immigration, its economy gathering steam after a serious downturn – but where it was headed was not so clear.

The wire blazer crest worn by members of the Canadian Legion, British Empire Service League, from its formation in 1926 featured a gold maple leaf on a Union Jack motif. In 1960, the organization was renamed the Royal Canadian Legion and adopted a new badge – after much debate – that did away with any reference to the British flag. But when Pearson pointed out to his Winnipeg audience that the Legion's new badge was designed around a red maple leaf on a white background, he was met with a chorus of boos.

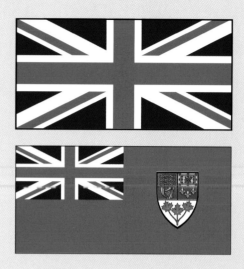

PARTS OF A FLAG

While flags can be sub-divided in many ways, they are usually thought of as being halved into the hoist (the half next to the flagpole) and the fly (the outer half). When these halves are themselves halved, they are called the upper hoist, the lower hoist, the upper fly and the lower fly. Of these four quadrants, the position of most importance is the upper hoist, known as the canton. In an ensign of British origin, like the Canadian Red Ensign (*above*), the canton is charged with a Union Jack.

BY 1964, Great Britain no longer ruled the waves or much else beyond the British Isles. Most of its former colonies had become independent or were in the process of becoming so, and its status as the world's greatest power was a distant memory. But the Union Jack still ruled many of the world's flags, including the national flags of Australia, New Zealand and, unofficially, Canada. These flags were British ensigns, usually in heraldic parlance "defaced" in the fly with an emblem particular to the place. Both Australia's and New Zealand's ensigns were defaced in the fly with stars representing the

constellation called the Southern Cross. Australia's flag also featured a seven-pointed star in the lower hoist meant to represent the Australian Commonwealth (one point for each of the six states and a seventh for the territories). The design for this star emerged from a national flag contest held in 1901 that garnered thirty thousand entries.

The Canadian Red Ensign began life as the flag of the British merchant marine. At Confederation in 1867, the official Canadian flag was the Royal Union flag, or Union Jack, but a Red Ensign defaced in the fly with the shield from the Canadian coat of arms soon became the de facto Canadian flag. After 1945, by federal order-in-council the Canadian Red Ensign was flown from all federal buildings in Canada and abroad "until such time as Parliament shall adopt a national flag."

One of the principal objections to an ensign as Canada's official flag was its similarity to all the other flags that already bore the Union Jack. During the Suez Crisis of 1956, Lester Pearson (then Canada's minister of external affairs) discovered first-hand how this sameness could pose a problem. Despite Canada's key role in brokering a ceasefire, Egypt's president, Gamal Abdel Nasser, objected to Canadian troops as part of the United Nations Emergency Force because of their British-looking flag. Pearson would refer to this lesson more than once during his 1964 flag quest.

Anguilla
Australia
Bermuda
British Antarctic Territory
British Indian Ocean Territory

British Virgin Islands
Cayman Islands
Cook Islands
Falkland Islands
Fiji

Gibraltar
Montserrat
New South Wales
New Zealand
Niue

Pitcairn Island
Saint Helena
South Georgia and South Sandwich Islands
Turks and Caicos Islands
Tuvalu

This anti-conscription rally in Quebec City during the First World War suggests the depth of the province's opposition to the 1917 passage of the Military Service Act by the Union government led by Prime Minister Robert Borden. Almost every French-speaking member of Parliament voted against the bill, including former prime minister Sir Wilfrid Laurier. Borden had invited Laurier to join the governing coalition, but the Liberal leader had refused, fearing a massive loss of support to Henri Bourassa and his *nationalistes*.

Canada had brains and energy to spare, but it was not quite sure just what those brains and that energy were for, what all its people, who came from so many different places and now mingled in towns and cities from coast to coast, added up to. What was this place called Canada? What did Canada stand for? And if that true identity were hoisted up a flagpole, how many would stand up and salute it?

Such questions of identity and nationhood were common then. Nearing the end of its tenth decade of existence, the country seemed mighty fragile. When Lester Pearson spoke to the legionnaires about the threat to Canada's survival he wasn't exaggerating. The unity crisis of the mid-1960s was just the latest in a series of set-tos between the two founding peoples, the French and the English, since Confederation in 1867, but the breakup of the country appeared to be a distinct possibility.

The young dominion had come perilously close to being torn apart in the 1890s following Sir John A. Macdonald's death. During his final years in office, the Old Chieftain had needed all his wiles to contain French-English animosity inflamed by the

execution of Louis Riel and, a few years later, by the removal of separate school rights from Manitoba's French-speaking Catholics. After Macdonald's passing, his electoral coalition fractured, and only Wilfrid Laurier's masterful manoeuvring averted a breakdown of the party system that could easily have led to a disconfederation of the founding provinces back into quarrelling colonies.

The next crisis came during the First World War, when Prime Minister Robert Borden enacted conscription and formed an Anglos-only Union government that included almost all his Conservatives and the bulk of Laurier's English-speaking Liberal caucus. The conscription crisis of the Second World War was less severe, thanks mostly to Prime Minister William Lyon Mackenzie King's adroit fence-sitting, epitomized by what has become the quintessential Canadian political pronouncement: "Conscription if necessary, but not necessarily conscription."

Since then Canada's two solitudes had been too busy making money and making babies to have much time for national crises. In Quebec this relative calm was greatly helped by the dominance of the reactionary

Union Nationale regime of Premier Maurice Duplessis, who had kept his province stuck in a kind of colonial time warp where the mother country had simply been replaced by the mother (Catholic) church. But Duplessis had died in 1959, and the upset victory of Jean Lesage and his Liberal Party in the provincial election of 1960 unleashed such a burst of modernizing energy that pundits called the rapid transformation of Quebec society "la Révolution tranquille," the Quiet Revolution.

Lesage's election also marked the reawakening of the forces of aggressive Quebec nationalism, more or less dormant since the 1920s when Abbé Lionel Groulx advocated his dream of a separate, French-speaking Laurentian state. With each passing year the Lesage government grew more assertive in its relations with Ottawa. Only a few weeks before Pearson flew to Winnipeg, Premier Lesage had hosted a federal-provincial conference in Quebec City at which he flatly refused to sign on to Pearson's cherished Canada Pension Plan. The most vivid expression of separatism's rise came courtesy of the Front de Libération du Québec (FLQ), whose program of

Taken together these three World War I recruiting posters encapsulate the divided identity of a proud English Canada that is also a loyal member of the British Empire. (*Left to right*) Imperial patriotism is foremost in this appeal to "Britons and Canadians" to "Fight Under Your Own Flag," that flag being the Union Jack. The middle poster sends a subtler message by waving the "Canadian" flag of the day, a Canadian Red Ensign, with its competing British and Canadian symbolism. The third and most Canadian of the three, with its direct appeal to Irish Canadians, employs only the home-grown maple leaf.

Overleaf: Graves in a cemetery in France memorialize Canadian soldiers who lost their lives in the final stages of the Battle of the Somme in November 1916.

In the first weeks after Pearson took over as prime minister from John Diefenbaker in April 1963, the separatist FLQ communicated its program of violent revolution loud and clear.

On April 20, a bomb at a Montreal armoury killed the night watchman, Wilfrid O'Neill. Less than a month later, on May 17, Sergeant Major Walter Leja of the RCMP was badly injured (*opposite above*) while attempting to defuse a bomb planted in a mailbox at the corner of Lansdowne and Westmount Avenues (*opposite below*), one of fourteen planted that day in Westmount mailboxes.

violent revolution had so far killed a night watchman at a Montreal armoury and set off a succession of explosions in symbolic strongholds of Anglo power, including mailboxes in Westmount, the bastion of Montreal's Anglo elite.

For many on both sides of the linguistic and racial divide, the flag issue became a focal point of the unity crisis. The legionnaire who shouted back at Mike Pearson, "You're selling us out to the pea-soupers," was not an isolated voice. He spoke for a huge segment of the anglophone population from coast to coast whose dislike and distrust of French Canadians in general and French-speaking Quebeckers in particular had been fed by generations of inbred prejudice. An English Canadian outside of Quebec who could speak French was a rare phenomenon; inside the province, it was almost as unusual.

For their part, French Canadians nurtured ancient enmities along with some very legitimate grievances. Symbolic of the state of affairs in the early 1960s was the frequently cited complaint that clerks at Eaton's department store in downtown Montreal spoke not a word of French, the first language of more than half their customers. On average, French Quebeckers earned considerably less than their English-speaking fellow citizens. The language of big business was English, and all the corporate head offices in Montreal were run by Anglos. Barriers to economic advancement were exemplified by Canadian National Railways president Donald Gordon's assertion before a House of Commons committee in 1962 that none of the many thousands of French Canadians in his employ was on the CNR board or in upper management because none of them was qualified. (The following day he was burned in effigy by student protesters in Montreal.)

Most French Canadians simply could not understand the attachment felt by *les Anglos* to what they viewed as colonial symbols: the Queen, the Union Jack. During an inconclusive flag debate back in 1946, a Quebec MP had sarcastically suggested, "We should keep the Union Jack, not because it is the flag of another country, but because it is a flag which is the emblem of the colonialism of a certain number of Canadians in public life. They are colonials. That is why they should keep the emblem of the empire. The Imperialists have no country."

In the 1960s, French Quebeckers increasingly felt that they did have a country – and it was not Canada. Few invested much emotional capital in the flag issue – except on one point: if there was going to be a new flag, it had better not include the Union Jack, the symbol of their conquest and their second-class citizenship.

In English Canada the flag question split people along demographic and ethnic lines. Canadians born before the Second World War tended to cling to the old flag, which for them was the Red Ensign. Canadians born since the war tended to favour something new, different, devoid of colonial imagery. And most of the one-third of Canadians who traced their lineage to neither France nor Britain wanted a flag that said Canada and nothing else.

In an urban riding like Ontario's Hamilton West, which was divided pretty evenly between those of Italian heritage and British heritage, this reality became starkly evident to the sitting member of Parliament as the flag issue heated up. Liberal Joe Macaluso

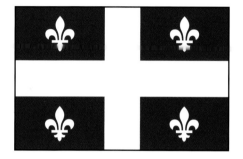

Many flags have flown over the territory now called Canada since Europeans first stepped ashore. One of the earliest known images of the British Red Ensign being used as the de facto Canadian flag appears in this landscape *(left)* by Robert Irvine, a Scottish-born employee of the North West Company who'd fought in the War of 1812. Irvine's *View of York*, painted around 1815, "sets the historical precedent for the flag as a symbol of claimed (or colonized) space," according to curator Anna Hudson of the Art Gallery of Ontario. In contrast, Quebec's familiar blue-and-white fleur-de-lys banner *(above)*, or *fleurdelisé*, might be described as an attempt to "reclaim conquered space." It was adopted by the Union Nationale government of Premier Maurice Duplessis in 1948, making it one of the earliest of Canada's provincial flags.

THE CANADIAN FLAG STORY really begins in the France and England of the Middle Ages, where the practice of heraldry grew out of the need for men in armour to distinguish friend from foe. The *herald* who announced the names of jousting champions evolved into the person who created *heraldic* devices that decorated a knight's armour, his shield and his personal battle stan-dard or gonfalon. Eventually certain standardized symbols, called devices, and certain colours came to be associated with certain groups. When overlaid with the crosses of one or another saint these often became the armorial bearings of noble or royal families. Thus the red cross of Saint George on a white background became the flag of the English kings. Three gold fleurs-de-lys on a blue field came to represent the royal family of France.

The Canadian coat of arms (here pictured in its current form) provides a lesson in contemporary heraldry. It is derived from the royal arms of Great Britain and contains many similar elements: for example, the wreath beneath the scroll contains English roses, Scots thistles and Irish shamrocks (the French lilies are a Canadian embellishment). The "full achievement" of armorial bearings has four parts: arms (the devices that appear on the shield), crest (the devices that sit atop the shield), supporters (the devices that support the shield) and motto (words that can appear above or below the whole). The arms of Canada combine the traditional emblems of British royalty – the three lions passant of England, the lion rampant of Scotland, the stringed harp of Ireland, the three fleurs-de-lys of France – with Canada's unique heraldic signature, three red maple leaves "conjoined on one stem proper." In 1994, the circlet ribbon was added, bearing the motto of the Order of Canada.

Canada has two official banners in addition to its national flag: the Queen's personal Canadian banner of arms bearing her cypher (*above left*) and the flag of the governor general (*above right*).

(who would soon be called to serve on the Flag Committee) remembers that nearly all the protests and complaints about Mr. Pearson and his maple leaf flag came from the Anglo south end. Most of the Italians in the north end of his constituency were in favour.

When you added these New Canadians, as they were still known, to younger-generation Canadians and sympathetic French-speakers, the result was a strong majority in favour of Pearson's flag crusade. It helped, too, that the notion of an all-new flag caught something of the spirit of the times.

In the mid-1960s, Canadian politicians were racing to catch up with their changing country in a time of unprecedented social and intellectual ferment. A cute British pop group called the Beatles had just burst onto the scene. "The pill" was about to transform sexual morality. The Vietnam War was already beginning to radicalize a whole generation of North American students. Revolution was in the air, and not just in *la belle province*. Remaking Western society seemed entirely possible, even desirable. In the 1960s many young people really believed that they could change the world for the

better. In Canada many of them thought the maple leaf flag seemed like a good idea simply because it was completely different and annoyed their parents. But it also came to represent for some of them what their country could become.

Quite a few – mostly young – Canadians believed that a new kind of country was in the process of being born, one that would bury the prejudices of the past deep under permafrost. They instantly understood – perhaps better than Pearson himself – the dream of Canada that transcended racial and religious divisions, that abandoned parochialism but honoured both its founding cultures while elevating its newest citizens to equal status with them. Some of them were young English Canadians who strove to learn French, participated in student exchanges with schools in Quebec and struggled to master the *joual* dialogue in contemporary Quebec novels, as they sought to understand "what Quebec wants." They and their soulmates in Quebec imagined Canada as a bilingual, bicultural promised land.

LESTER PEARSON FLEW HOME from Winnipeg to Ottawa basking in a glow of

The first Great Seal of Canada (*above*), which was in use from 1869 until 1904, is the third of Canada's symbols of sovereignty (the others are the national flag and the national coat of arms). Canada's first great seal established the custom of picturing the enthroned Canadian monarch, in this case Queen Victoria. She holds an orb and sceptre and is flanked by the coats of arms of the four original provinces. The arms of Canada are at her feet. Canada's great seals were all manufactured by the Royal Mint in London until the accession of Queen Elizabeth II in 1952.

When Canada Post released its Unity issue just before Pearson's trip to Winnipeg, many assumed its design was the prime minister's personal choice for the new flag.

achievement. Historian J.L. Granatstein has described him as "a man who believed that everything he did was right and necessary," who pursued his goals with a "sometimes frightening and total self-confidence," which was often at odds with his fumbling public persona. For once, however, his private sense was matched by his public performance. He'd wrestled with the demons of opposition and won. Mind you, the fight always seemed easier when he was outside the House of Commons and away from his nemesis, John Diefenbaker. Now the question in the public's mind was: Precisely which distinctive flag would the prime minister present to Parliament?

Being a diplomat by training and instinct, Pearson would opt for a compromise designed to offend the fewest and to please the most. For several months it had been quite clear from his public statements that the prime minister favoured a flag that bore a maple leaf or leaves, without either of the traditional symbols: the Union Jack or the fleur-de-lys. The PM's chosen design remained a mystery to just about everyone until a few days before his Winnipeg speech, even though he and John Matheson had been working on it for some months.

In early March, Matheson had introduced Pearson to his old friend Alan Beddoe, a retired navy lieutenant-commander and graphic artist with a solid knowledge of heraldry. At their meeting, Pearson asked Beddoe to prepare some possible designs for his consideration. Beddoe was no stranger to this sort of commission, having designed over 180 of the emblems worn by vessels in the Royal Canadian Navy during the Second World War as well as the recently adopted maple leaf insignia of the Royal Canadian Legion.

Matheson made clear to Beddoe what his draft designs should be based on. His own heraldic research had led him swiftly and sensibly to a simple conclusion: the right flag for Canada would consist of "a white field charged with three red maple leaves conjoined on a single stem." Why so? Because three stylized red sugar maple leaves on one stem against a white background formed "the Canadian component of Canada's shield," which was the central element in the Canadian coat of arms granted to Canada by King George V in 1921. It did not hurt that the maple leaf had been used both formally and informally as a Canadian emblem as far

back as the early 1800s and possibly before. Matheson knew the idea for a three-maple-leaf flag was not new. It had first been proposed by Colonel A. Fortescue Duguid, a heraldic expert who had served for many years as the chief historian of the general staff at National Defence Headquarters. Matheson also believed strongly that this design was heraldically the purest.

One Saturday morning in early May, a week or so before the prime minister's Winnipeg speech, Beddoe and Matheson arrived for an appointment at 24 Sussex Drive, the prime minister's official residence. Pearson greeted them warmly and ushered them into his study. Beddoe dutifully produced several variant designs with red leaves on white. "Then, without any prior advice or warning," Matheson recalled, "Beddoe extracted from his briefcase another design, with vertical blue bars, which he handed to the prime minister saying: 'Perhaps you would prefer this flag which conveys the message: From Sea to Sea.'" (Beddoe had been keeping a very similar design in his drawer for a decade; he had sent it to Prime Minister Louis St. Laurent in 1955.)

Those opposed to Pearson's flag initiative called for the government to hold a national plebiscite on the issue. Here John Dalrymple of the Emergency Committee to Save the Red Ensign displays a pro-referendum petition containing six thousand signatures and stretching 125 feet in length.

John Matheson displays Alan Beddoe's three-maple-leaf design. More than any other person, Matheson had devoted himself to the quest for a distinct Canadian flag. He'd begun researching flags and teaching himself heraldry while the Liberals were still in opposition. On February 5, 1963, he asked two loaded questions in the House. The first: "Does Canada have national colours and, if so, what are those colours?" The government replied, "Yes, white and red." The second: "Does Canada have a national emblem, and, if so, what is the emblem?" The government answered, "Yes, three maple leaves conjoined on one stem." Matheson would have preferred a simple white flag with three red leaves, but Pearson liked Beddoe's blue bars and so this variation became his government's choice.

Matheson was appalled. Pearson was "enchanted." The Beddoe design was attractive, the addition of bright blue bands made it more lively and prettier up close, and the sea-to-sea motif resonated with Pearson's desire to promote Canadian unity. Matheson bit his tongue. He could have pointed out that vertical blue bars do not indicate water in the lexicon of heraldic imagery; water is indicated by a wavy fess, an undulating horizontal bar. But he realized that such objections would seem silly. Pearson had found what he wanted: a compromise he believed he could sell to his cabinet and to the Canadian people.

On May 14, only two days before the Winnipeg trip, Pearson floated two trial balloons, both bearing a sprig of three red maple leaves. That morning the post office released a new five-cent postage stamp that showed the red leaves on a light blue background. Just before six o'clock that evening, the prime minister summoned eight members of the Parliamentary Press Gallery to a private flag briefing at 24 Sussex Drive. As they relaxed over drinks and sandwiches, "Mr. Pearson brought

out several flag designs on cardboard," wrote Val Sears of the *Toronto Star*, "selected one with a cluster of three maple leaves and two blue bands and placed it on the mantelpiece as his choice. He said he was prepared to have the government stand or fall on the maple leaf flag."

Sears was not alone in wondering at the wisdom of the prime minister's strategy as he and the other reporters wrote their stories describing Pearson's "personal choice." By the time the PM hopped on the plane for Winnipeg, anyone who'd been reading the newspapers had a good idea of what he had in mind. At a press conference immediately following the speech, he erased all doubts by showing the western press corps his preferred design.

As a demonstration of how Pearson operated, the maple leaf flag makes a good case study. He had proceeded with the flag brief despite considerable disquiet in his cabinet and over the objections of his closest advisers, who wanted the government to regroup from the shambles of its "Sixty Days of Decision," which had culminated in Finance Minister Walter Gordon being forced to withdraw his first budget.

SATURDAY · MARCH 7

Picked John Matheson up at his office at 9.am and after a chat on the tactics we should adopt we went to the PM's residence on Sussex Drive for a meeting at 10.am.

Mr Pearson was waiting and after preliminaries we got down to the subject of the Flag. John was disappointed with the meeting; he felt the PM had other things on his mind & was only making a feeble attempt to come to real grips with the problem. Mr P did however ask me to prepare some designs. He is apparently sold on the 'Maple Leaves' but it is quite obvious he has not yet acquired a correct understanding or appreciation of the principles that are involved in the design of a Flag for Canada.

SUNDAY · MARCH 8

Poor John was very depressed over the result of the interview, but I tried to convince him that it was not as bad as he believed. Mr. Pearson asked us to meet with him again in three weeks time when I will have some designs to submit.

———

Sunday March 8ᵗʰ

A day of rest and meditation. Pattie came out for dinner & brought with her Muriel Deeks — & 'Dormey' of course.

Graphic artist Alan Brookman Beddoe (pictured below working on the Book of Remembrance not long after the Second World War) had made Canadian flags and Canadian heraldry his passion. Unknown to either Matheson or Pearson, in September 1955 Beddoe had developed a design (*above*) very similar to the one he presented to the prime minister in May 1964. He included this earlier flag proposal in a letter to Prime Minister Louis St. Laurent, dated September 20, 1955. St. Laurent, who was not one for rocking the boat, replied politely and filed the letter away. During Beddoe's intensive involvement in helping develop Canada's national flag in 1964, he kept a diary. The entry for March 7 (*left*) recounts his first meeting with Pearson and provides a wonderfully human glimpse behind the scenes.

On June 1, a large group of mostly young adherents of the Pearson Pennant gathered on the west lawn of Parliament Hill to demonstrate. An opposing crowd, mostly older, occupied the east lawn and waved the Red Ensign. The blue-and-red three-leaf flags on the west lawn showed all sorts of variations on Alan Beddoe's original design, which Pearson had revealed as the government's choice after the cabinet meeting on May 26. Not only was this design constantly changing (the blue bars getting wider or narrower, the original bulges in the three stems smoothed out), but Pearson had done nothing to control its reproduction. Anyone who wanted to make a Pearson flag could and, it seemed, did.

This is the version of the Pearson Pennant that was given to every member of Parliament and every senator on May 27, 1964.

The prime minister made his personal choice and made it public before consulting anyone other than John Matheson and Alan Beddoe. By the time he presented it to his cabinet colleagues it was for all practical purposes a *fait accompli.*

On May 19, the day Pearson returned from Winnipeg, he emerged from a cabinet meeting to announce that he and his colleagues had unanimously agreed that the Red Ensign should be replaced by a flag sporting a maple leaf motif. Two days later, the cabinet met and picked the design the prime minister wanted: three red leaves on white flanked by two vertical blue bars. On May 27, Pearson formally unfurled his proposed flag design. That day every one of the 263 members of Parliament and all 98 senators found a full-colour rendering of the Pearson flag tucked into their daily sheaf of documents.

The responses, both pro and con, were immediate, plentiful, often passionate – and confusing. John Diefenbaker predictably condemned the design, dismissing it as "Pearson's pennant" (a nickname that stuck) and calling for a national plebiscite on the flag issue. Diefenbaker seems

to have believed truly and deeply that Pearson's choice was wrong in every way. No better summary of his attitude can be found than a memo discovered in his personal flag files and heavily underscored in pencil by him. It reads: "The Pearson Flag is a meaningless Flag. There is no recognition of history; no indication of the existence of French and English Canada; the partnership of the races; no acknowledgement of history. It is a flag without a past, without history, without honour and without pride." One of Dief's favourite ploys in the days that followed was to cite the Molson Canadian beer label and to ask if the same person who had designed the label had designed the flag. Another was to inform his listeners that since 1956 the sugar maple had been the official tree of New York State. He could also gleefully report that the Communist Party of Canada had sent a telegram to Pearson supporting his pennant. The Chief had a field day with the flag.

The other opposition parties were generally on Pearson's side, though unsure his specific proposal represented the ideal design. New Democrat leader Tommy Douglas expressed his party's willingness

to back the prime minister's choice; a member of his caucus, Reid Scott, proposed a single-maple-leaf version of the Pearson Pennant as his personal preference. Réal Caouette, leader of the Ralliement des Créditistes (which had recently broken away from the western flank of the Social Credit Party), wanted a flag divided diagonally into red and white halves with a green maple leaf in the middle, but allowed he would go along with the prime minister's design if he had to. In sum, if the measure ever came to a vote, it would pass handily.

But a number of provincial premiers expressed their opposition, among them Socred W.A.C. Bennett of British Columbia, Tory John Robarts of Ontario and Liberal Joey Smallwood of Newfoundland. Smallwood promised, "Newfoundland will continue to fly the Union Jack if we are the last people on earth to do so." But former Diefenbaker cabinet minister George Hees, president of the Montreal and Canadian Stock Exchanges, stuck a knife in the Chief's back by championing Pearson's choice. The Canadian Chamber of Commerce quickly announced its support. A number of individual Legion chapters

continued to fly the Red Ensign in public protest, but many of the hundreds of thousands of veterans who didn't belong to the Legion voiced their support. And ordinary Canadians from every province expressed their approval or their outrage in letters to the editor or to their MP.

During the months since Pearson had made his flag intentions clear, members of Parliament had been receiving design proposals from the general public. More of them flooded in over the next six months, bringing the total to several thousand. Organizations sprang up to "save the Red Ensign," including one backed by the still-active Imperial Order Daughters of the Empire. Typical of these grassroots uprisings was the Red Ensign Club of Canada, British Columbia Division, which aired the usual arguments about history and tradition along with a religious reason for keeping the flag: "The Red Ensign Represents Christian Values." And was Canada not a Christian country? Another favourite objection voiced in editorials and opinion columns, especially west of Ontario, was that the sugar maple tree didn't grow anywhere west of the Ontario-Manitoba border.

Pearson's executive assistant, Richard O'Hagan, hands the prime minister the two flag designs he had shown to the press after his Winnipeg speech. These were only two of some three hundred being considered, Pearson told the reporters, before adding cagily that these were two of the most favoured. The upper design was an early version of the Pearson Pennant. The lower, three red maple leaves on a white field, was the version favoured by John Matheson as being the most correct heraldically.

In late May, a group of
students from the Uni-
versity of Toronto pre-
sented Prime Minister
Pearson with a petition
backing his proposal for
a maple leaf flag (*opposite*).
Public support for the
Pearson Pennant was

running strong, and it
began to look like the
flag might become law
in time for the Queen's
visit in October. A Gallup
poll published on June 5
found that 63 percent
of urban Canadians
favoured the Pearson

Pennant. But the prime
minister created a par-
liamentary uproar on
June 12 when he had the
proposed flag run up a
specially constructed
flagpole on Parliament
Hill. When one NDP
member of Parliament

broke through the crowd
to protest at the flying of
an "unauthorized flag,"
he was drowned out by a
chorus of Quebec Liberals
singing "O Canada." It was
a taste of parliamentary
broils to come.

Professional artists and designers took great pleasure in panning Pearson's flag. The principal of the Ontario College of Art told a reporter, "If a student submitted this design with his application to enter the college, he wouldn't be admitted ... The maple leaf can't be used to make a good design. It's impossible to handle." Artist Jack Shadbolt commented from Vancouver, "It's a poor, crowded design, with two of the leaves jammed down, making the corners look ragged. When this flag is furled there will be nothing but jagged pieces of colour to show what it is." His Toronto confrere Harold Town suggested the best place for the Pearson Pennant was the garbage can. And a *New York Times* editorial patronizingly called it "the charming flag that Mr. Pearson supports," going on to say that its colour scheme made it "seem more French than British." Just what Pearson needed.

It seemed as if everybody had an opinion, including a number of distinguished academics. A group of them, led by Donald Creighton and Eugene Forsey, wrote a strongly worded letter to the prime minister, in which they began by agreeing an official flag was a good idea, assuming it

was unmistakably Canadian and a unifying force: "However, we protest that the maple leaf flag is neither of these things. Its only advantage is that it is innocuous, that it produces tepid approval, mild disapproval, or indifference, that it can therefore be adopted without any display of strong feeling whatever. We have a despairing feeling that this insipid flag, instead of promoting national unity, will produce only an indifferent response, and in doing so will subtly undermine the Canadian will to survive."

Like Diefenbaker and a host of others, these scholars believed "the very essence of this country's history, and the reason for our national distinctiveness, has been the long and often turbulent marriage of French and English heritages." Only a flag that wedded these two traditions in some suitably symbolic way made any sense to them.

But Pearson's pretty red, white and blue flag pleased greater numbers than it offended. Soon versions of it began to appear in towns and cities across the land – and even in New York, where Delmonico's Hotel on Park Avenue flew a Pearson Pennant

above the front entrance. Because Pearson hadn't thought to control the precise design, these flags varied widely – from versions with thin blue bands and big red leaves to versions with wide blue bands and tiny leaves. By early June, Pearson Pennants sprouted from car aerials and hung from apartment balconies and were worn in provocative positions by striptease artists or bikini-clad sunbathers. The flag issue had clearly caught the public imagination. But from every second flagpole the Red Ensign flapped stubbornly in the warm spring breezes.

On June 13, the government tabled its flag motion in the House of Commons. On June 15, the Flag Debate began with a parliamentary haggle over Diefenbaker's demand that the motion be split into two separate propositions, one adopting the maple leaf flag, the second making the Union Jack the flag of the Commonwealth. After Speaker Alan Macnaughton ruled in favour of dividing the motion, Prime Minister Pearson rose from his seat on the front bench to lead off the debate. His eloquent and carefully argued speech represents one of the few moments of

NDP leader Tommy Douglas (*above left, speaking to reporters*) and Tory leader John Diefenbaker both came from the Prairies and knew how to spellbind an audience. Ideologically, however, they differed deeply, as they did on the flag question. Like Diefenbaker, Douglas carried a sentimental attachment to the Red Ensign, but he accepted Pearson's choice. "The fact is that my children couldn't care less whether the Union Jack is on it or the fleur-de-lys is on it," he told an audience. "They're Canadians and their children are Canadians and this flag is not for today and tomorrow. This flag is for a hundred years, we hope five hundred years from now."

sanity in what would turn out to be a bitter, six-month parliamentary marathon.

Pearson built his case carefully and cogently, mixing reason with passion. He spent a good deal of time establishing the historical precedent for the maple leaf as a distinctly Canadian symbol with origins predating Confederation, and he paid particular attention to its use as an army badge in the First and Second World Wars. In closing, he quoted a translation of the Latin inscription on the monument to James Wolfe and the Marquis de Montcalm, the British and French generals who had both died at the Battle of the Plains of Abraham in 1759, the event that symbolized Britain's conquest of New France:

> Valour gave them a common death
> History a common fame
> Posterity a common monument
>> Mr. Speaker, it is for this generation, for this Parliament, to give them and give us all a common flag; a Canadian flag which, while bringing together but rising above the landmarks and milestones of the past, will say proudly to the world and to the future: "I stand for Canada."

The prime minister sat down as the Liberal ranks rose and cheered. Applause came also from many members of the New Democratic Party and from the Créditistes. Perhaps more than a scattering of the Tories who sat behind the grim-faced front bench clapped in their imaginations. Then John Diefenbaker rose, jowls quivering, eyes blazing, hand on hip in a classic courtroom pose. He waited until the hubbub had subsided. The first of his interminable sentences rolled forth, and any hope that Pearson's charming red, blue and white flag might briefly unite Canada's political factions in pursuit of a higher purpose was dashed for good.

"There was no mention in all of his speech of the contribution of the people of French origin in our country. There was no mention of the contribution made by Sir George-Étienne Cartier, with Macdonald, to the bringing about of Confederation. This was a significant omission in every part of his remarks. As he concluded ... that our purpose in this nation should be to build unity and to avoid dissension, I say to the Prime Minister this, Physician, heal thyself. You have brought in, at a time when there are many other matters that ought to have received the consideration of the House, this question that cannot have any other effect than to divide this nation as it has not been divided."

JOHN GEORGE DIEFENBAKER, as leader of the opposition, replies to Lester Pearson's speech opening the Flag Debate, June 15, 1964

CHAPTER TWO

Badge of honour

BY THE WARM June day when Lester Pearson stood in the House of Commons to begin debate on his government's proposal for a national flag, the notion that this flag would bear a maple leaf, or leaves, as its primary symbol was taken for granted. By 1964, the maple leaf was so widely accepted as a distinctly Canadian emblem that all other candidates – including its closest rival, the earnest and industrious beaver – didn't stand a chance. But how and when did the maple leaf gain this special status?

Part of the answer lies in unrecorded social history, in the early interactions between European newcomers and Canada's indigenous peoples. It would be convenient if these new arrivals had encountered a cult of the maple leaf that they could adapt to their own purposes – as the descendants of the Spanish conquistadors adopted the sacred bird of the Aztecs, the quetzal, as the national bird of Guatemala. But apart from a scattering of surviving artifacts made by the forest-dwelling inhabitants of north-eastern North America, which incorporate a maple leaf or leaves in decorative ways, we have almost nothing to go on.

There is an Ojibway legend explaining why the sugar maple tree's sap runs thin. Once upon a time, the story goes, the maple's sap was thick and syrupy, allowing the people of the forest to lounge around and do nothing much but drink the maple nectar. When this sorry state of affairs came to the attention of the trickster-hero Nanabozho (also Manabozho or Nana-bush), he climbed to the top of each maple tree and poured in bucket after bucket of water until the sap turned thin and watery and not nearly so sweet. He also declared that the sap would run for only a few weeks each year. That way human beings couldn't depend on it all the time and would have to sweat a little before it became useful food. The legend is a moral lesson about the value of hard work and an indicator of the economic value the Ojibway placed on sugar maple sap – a value the outsiders soon learned – but it does nothing to endow the sugar maple's leaf with special status. When the early settlers encountered the pretty foliage that turned bright scarlet as the days shortened toward winter, it was simply that: a strikingly attractive leaf. Yet somewhere along the line between first contact and Confederation, the maple leaf

In the Second World War, everywhere Canadian troops went, there went the maple leaf – including on this Spitfire of 402 Squadron RCAF flown by Norm Bretz (*opposite*).

PINNING THEIR HOPES ON THE MAPLE LEAF

Great waves of immigration helped Canada's population to grow from 5.4 million to 7.2 million between 1901 and 1911, an increase of almost 35 percent. The newcomers displayed a strong desire to fit into their adopted homeland. Many of them bought pins and brooches boasting Canadian emblems – federal and provincial crests, for instance – crafted by jewellery makers in Montreal and Toronto. A great number of these patriotic keepsakes bore the maple leaf, which came to represent the promise of a freer and more prosperous life. The pins and brooches were colourful items, often made of sterling silver or copper and sometimes enamelled.

John Cabot probably planted the royal banner of King Henry VII somewhere along what is now Newfoundland's east coast on June 24, 1497 (St. John the Baptist Day), thereby asserting the king's sovereignty over the unknown country. This banner, with its English lions and French lilies, could easily have been proposed as a design for Canada's national flag during the flag debates of the 1960s.

– among all the possible indigenous plants and animals and crafted objects – came to be thought of as the primary Canadian emblem, the image that meant Canada.

The idea that a picture of an eagle, a laurel branch, a lion or a lotus flower could represent something much more than itself – a military unit, a family, a business enterprise, a tribe – is very old indeed and existed in North America before the arrival of the European interlopers. In the territory that is now Canada, the most striking expression of humanity's innate symbolic urge took the form of the elaborately carved poles of the Pacific Coast peoples, whose highly stylized representations of birds, fish and mammals collectively stood for the complex family histories of entire clans.

By the time the first outsider since Norse wayfarer Leif Ericsson bumped into a part of what is now Canada, the idea that an emblem could denote sovereignty was well established. In the early summer of 1497, when Giovanni Caboto (better known to our history books as John Cabot) stepped ashore on the coast of Newfoundland (or maybe Labrador, or perhaps Cape Breton), he was looking for a shorter shipping route

to the Far East. But he made sure to claim the bleak and rocky place for his employer, King Henry VII of England, and called it New Found Land. The flag Cabot planted was not, as is often supposed, the banner of Saint George, England's patron saint, which bore a red cross on a white field. The one he brought ashore was the king's royal banner, which copied the four quarters of the shield of the Tudor coat of arms: in the upper left and lower right, three gold fleurs-de-lys on a blue (azure) field; in the upper right and lower left, three gold lions rampant on a red field. This heraldic scheme neatly expressed the king's claim of dominion over large parts of France as well as England. Cabot also raised a large wooden cross. He thus symbolically took possession of this newly discovered country on behalf of a Christian king who asserted his authority over England and much of France – a nice omen, considering the future interweaving of our two "founding peoples."

Fewer than fifty years later, in the summer of 1534, and several hundred kilometres to the west at what is now Gaspé Harbour, a similar ceremony unfolded, but with a Gallic accent.

In one form or another the maple leaf appeared with increasing frequency during Canada's early years. Each of these two Blackfoot elders (*below right*), photographed in the 1930s by Arnold Lupson of Calgary, has a beadwork maple leaf on his chest. When it came to costuming "Our Lady of the Snows" for a stereopticon image of Canadian femininity in 1909 (*bottom*), the model's ensemble simply had to include a maple leaf pullover. (The phrase "Our Lady of the Snows" as a metaphor for Canada was coined by Rudyard Kipling.)

16265—"Our Lady of the Snows"—A Strictly Canadian Character

As long as there have been Canadian coins, some have been decorated with maple leaves. Until 1937, the first full year of George VI's reign, all Canada's metal currency bore a leaf design on the side called the reverse and a portrait of the reigning sovereign on the side called the obverse. That year, to accompany the new king's portrait, the reverse side of all of Canada's coins was re-designed. Since then and except for special issues – for example, to mark the 1967 centennial of Con-federation – these coins have stayed essentially the same, with the mon-arch on one side and an emblematic animal or object on the other. The penny has stayed true to the maple leaf for close to 150 years.

The earliest Canadian one-cent pieces were the large pennies issued before Confederation by the Province of Canada. So many were in circula-tion in 1867 that not until 1876 was the first true Canadian penny issued. From 1876 until 1920 the design on the reverse continued to feature the same serpentine wreath of maple leaves seen on the examples from 1890 (*left*) and 1897 (*above, far left*). On the obverse the young Queen Victoria gradually aged until she was replaced by her son Edward VII. In 1920, to save costs, the penny was reduced to its present size.

When the Société Saint-Jean-Baptiste was founded in Montreal in 1834, the fur trade still flourished, so it was natural that the society would place a beaver at the centre of its new logo. But from the beginning the organization dedicated to nurturing nationalist feeling, protecting Québécois language and culture, and promoting the Roman Catholic religion, associated itself with the maple leaf.

Here is Jacques Cartier's own account of the event.

"On Friday the twenty-fourth of the said month of July, we had a cross made thirty feet high, which we put together in the presence of a number of Indians on the point at the entrance to the harbour, under the cross-bar of which we fixed a shield with three fleurs-de-lys in relief, and above it a wooden board, engraved in large Gothic characters, where was written, VIVE LE ROY DE FRANCE… And when it had been raised in the air, we all knelt down with our hands joined." Cartier's gold lilies on their blue field signified the claim of his king, François I, to the unknown land.

These two contending claims set in motion the two-century-long competition between England and France for control of the New World's northern hemisphere, a contest settled militarily in 1759 at the Battle of the Plains of Abraham. Which brings us to the next chapter in our story – the one that takes us from Conquest to Confederation. It is here that the maple leaf emerges as a character big enough to take on the lions rampant, the royal fleur-de-lys and the Christian crosses, but as yet one without a distinct personality or any official authority.

Legend has it that as early as 1700, or even earlier, the *habitants* of New France were using maple leaves as symbols. But not until June 24, 1836, when the president of the young Société Saint-Jean-Baptiste, Denis-Benjamin Viger, in his address to the society's third annual banquet called for the maple leaf to become Canada's emblem, does this native plant officially enter the symbol sweepstakes.

"This tree, which grows in our valleys, on our rocks, at first young and beaten by the storm, is not vigorous, feeding itself with great difficulty from the soil. But soon it grows fast, and when it is tall and strong, does not fear storms and overcomes the North wind which is unable to shake it. The maple is the king of our forest; it is the emblem of the Canadian people."

The society subsequently adopted as its emblem a beaver encircled with maple leaves and bearing the motto: "Our Institutions, Our Language and Our Laws."

The same year, Viger's championing of the maple leaf was echoed by the Quebec City journal *Le Canadien*, which already featured a maple leaf on its masthead.

The original masthead of Montreal's *Canadian Illustrated News*, which features a beaver encircled by a wreath of maple leaves, is further evidence of the spread of the native emblem among English-speaking Canadians. This first issue of October 29, 1869, also happens to reaffirm the devotion of *les Anglos* to the British connection. It features a William Notman portrait photograph of Edward, Prince of Wales. The eight-page weekly's lavish illustrations make it seem closer to a twentieth-century newsmagazine than to the typical newspaper of its day. But then its founder, Georges E. Desbarats, was also co-inventor with William Auguste Leggo of a printing method for pictures known as Leggotype. *The Canadian Illustrated News* and its French sibling *L'Opinion publique* were positioned as popular, family newspapers. "By picturing to our own people the broad dominion they possess," wrote Desbarats, "its resources and progress, its monuments and industry, its great men and great events, such a paper would teach them to know and love it better, and by it they would learn to feel still prouder of the proud Canadian name."

Le Canadien proposed that a maple leaf insignia would make a suitable Canadian emblem. And in 1838 the Banque du Peuple de Montréal issued a one-sou coin with a maple leaf on one of its faces – the precursor of today's maple leaf penny. As all these examples confirm, in its earliest uses, the sugar maple leaf was a *Canadien* emblem.

Soon, however, maple leaves began sprouting throughout Upper Canada, neither the first nor the last time that English Canadians would adopt French-Canadian symbols as their own, thereby robbing them of their specifically *Canadien* connotation. And given English Canadians' overwhelming sense of belonging to something called Greater Britain, it is hardly surprising that the main maple leaf milestones marking the history of English-speaking Canada in the years up to Confederation (and for quite a while after) come to us with an Imperial tinge.

In August 1860, the loyal citizens of what was known as Upper Canada prepared to give Albert Edward, Prince of Wales (the future Edward VII), a royal welcome. (Upper Canada and Lower Canada had become the Province of Canada in 1841.) Many were equally determined to show off their Canadian identity. On August 21, St. Lawrence Hall in Toronto was nearly filled with those "anxious to take measures with a view to native Canadians taking part with distinctive badges in the procession on the occasion of the arrival of the Prince of Wales in Toronto," reported the Toronto *Globe*. "The greater proportion of those present were young men, natives of Canada, but there were also not a few well advanced in years, born in Upper Canada soon after its first settlement."

Once the meeting was called to order and a chairman and secretary appointed, the assembly turned smartly to its main business: "Mr. J. H. Morris moved the first resolution as follows: – 'That the Committee on the Programme having assigned to native Canadians a place in the procession in honour of His Royal Highness the Prince of Wales, it is desirable to take such steps as may be necessary for the effective organization of that part of it.'" He and his Canadian-born fellow citizens "wished simply by wearing the 'Maple Leaf,' on the day of the arrival of the Prince, to show that they were Native Canadians – (loud applause) –

ACCORDING TO LEGEND, Alexander Muir (*bottom right*) was inspired to compose "The Maple Leaf Forever," his ode to the newborn Dominion of Canada, while contemplating the majestic sugar maple that grew in the front yard of his property in Leslieville, now part of the City of Toronto. The song gained instant popularity in English Canada.

OUR EMBLEM DEAR

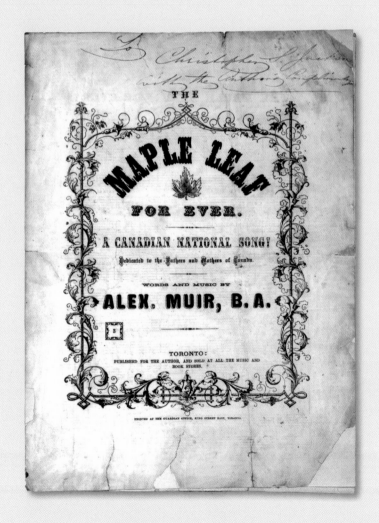

In days of yore
From Britain's shore
Wolfe the dauntless hero came
And planted firm Britannia's flag
On Canada's fair domain.
Here may it wave,
Our boast and pride,
And join in love together,
With thistle, shamrock, rose entwine
The Maple Leaf forever.

The Maple Leaf,
Our emblem dear,
The Maple Leaf forever.
God save our Queen and heaven bless
The Maple Leaf forever!

At Queenston Heights and Lundy's Lane
Our brave fathers side by side
For freedom, home and loved ones dear
Firmly stood and nobly died.
And those dear rights which they maintained
We swear to yield them never.
Our watchword ever more shall be:
The Maple Leaf forever.

Our fair Dominion now extends
From Cape Race to Nootka Sound.
May peace forever be our lot
And plenteous store abound.
And may those ties of love be ours
Which discord cannot sever,
And flourish green o'er freedom's home
The Maple Leaf forever.

This was the personal standard George Simpson flew as ruler of the vast dominion controlled by the Hudson's Bay Company (HBC) from 1821, when the company absorbed the rival North West Company, until his death in 1860. It bears the HBC governor's coat of arms, which dates to the company's founding in 1670. According to the original charter, each time the king or one of his heirs visited HBC territory, the governor was to present a tribute of "two Elks and two Black beavers." On the coat of arms we see these animals (the elks supporting the shield and four beavers quartering the shield) along with a single fox (atop the shield). The company motto, *Pro Pelle Cutem*, a play on the biblical maxim, "an eye for an eye," makes no sense when translated literally as "a skin for a pelt." Peter C. Newman, in his popular history of the HBC, explains it this way: "The original saying was probably intended to convey the risks incurred by the early adventurers, as in 'we risk our skins to get your pelts.'"

Around 1910, horses on show at the Victoria Provincial Exhibition in British Columbia wore this upside-down maple leaf emblem slipped into their bridles so that their prize ribbons could be suitably displayed. (Note the beaver perched on the base of the leaf.)

to be known to the world as such and as loyal subjects of Her Majesty. (Cheers)."

Such was the enthusiasm in the hall that the meeting quickly voted in favour of Mr. Morris's resolution, then adopted two others: "All Native Canadians joining the process, whether identified with the National Societies or not, should wear the maple leaf as an emblem of the land of their birth" and "The first public act of His Royal Highness having been the presentation of their banners to our noble Hundredth Regiment, he would doubtless also have the pleasure of sanctioning the adoption of the maple leaf as our national emblem."

The native-born burghers of Toronto were not alone in greeting the eldest son of Queen Victoria and Prince Albert with the sign of the maple leaf. The prince encountered it wherever he travelled in what is now Ontario. Many of the women who welcomed him wore lovely silver maple leaf brooches, and virtually every ceremonial arch and reviewing stand was festooned with maple leaves.

This Upper Canadian marriage of an indigenous symbol with Imperial pride found its perfect expression in 1868, when a school principal, Alexander Muir, published his Confederation song, "The Maple Leaf Forever." In some parts of English Canada, the song was still being taught and sung in the 1970s, even though "O Canada" had become the de facto national anthem in 1967 when Parliament passed a resolution approving its use.

The maple leaf's only serious competition was the beaver, whose pelt had once been North America's most valuable commodity. In 1673, Governor Frontenac of New France proposed the beaver as an emblem for the colony. In 1678, the Hudson's Bay Company was granted a coat of arms in which a beaver occupied each of the four quarters of the shield; it still adorns every Bay store in the country. In 1792, the paper money issued by the Canada Bank bore a beaver. In 1833, the port city of Montreal, in honour of the trade in pelts that had made it great, gave the beaver a proud place on its armorial bearings.

By Confederation, however, the beaver was already in a fast fade, along with the fortunes of the fur trade. It had reached its peak in 1851, when it was featured on what would become the new country's first

A proud-looking Saint Jean Baptiste waves to a motley crowd of Canadian types, including an Indian chief and a lumberjack, in this 1903 cartoon that appeared in the Montreal periodical *Les Débats*. In the foreground a figure wearing a kilt and shouldering the Union Jack is dwarfed by a maple leaf banner that is remarkably similar to the flag chosen sixty years later. The kilted gentleman can be none other than Sir John A. Macdonald, who famously declared, "A British subject I was born, a British subject I will die." French-speaking Quebeckers at the turn of the nineteenth century were the strongest proponents of a distinct Canadian flag.

Notre Drapeau National

postage stamp, the Three-Pence Beaver, designed by Sandford Fleming, who would later propose a striking (but beaverless) design for a distinctly Canadian national flag. From time to time attempts were made to resurrect the beaver as a symbol equal to or above the others. A 1904 tract written by a French-Canadian priest, F.A. Baillargé, argued, "Le castor est au nombre de nos traditions populaires les plus universelles et les plus antiques" (the beaver is among the oldest and most universal of our popular traditions). Father Baillargé gave it equal status to the maple leaf on his *drapeau canadien-français.*

With hindsight, however, the beaver was in many ways lacking as a potential national symbol. Graphically it makes an awkward image. Apart from being regularly skinned for profit, it is most noted for its engineering prowess. (It survives on many of the badges of the construction brigades in the Canadian Corps of the First World War.) But the beaver is also a destructive creature, seen as a pest by those trying to clear and settle the land. It creates swamps where they are not wanted and consumes useful hardwood. The beaver will continue to earn its five cents' worth as long as the Hudson's Bay Company owns department stores and the Canadian mint keeps making nickels, but it long ago lost its national sheen. Besides, why would a self-respecting country adopt a rodent with buck teeth and an outlandish tail – a cartoon animal that, some allege, consumes its own testicles when threatened and occasionally forgets to get out of the way of a tree it has felled – as the image it projects to the world?

A far better homegrown emblem, surely, would have been the canoe, which the continent's original inhabitants paddled for purposes of commerce and of war, and without which the fur trade so crucial to the economy of the new land would have been impossible. Like the maple leaf, the canoe is indigenous and has a pleasing shape. And its significance is embedded deep within the Canadian psyche, both French and English. Few canoes would turn up on the thousands of designs Canadians submitted to their political representatives in 1964. Perhaps the canoe's shape disqualified it: without a paddler it looks as if it is going in both directions at once.

Railway builder Sandford Fleming, who also came up with the idea for standard time, put a beaver on the postage stamp he designed in 1851 for the new customs union of four of Britain's North American colonies – Canada (the union of Upper and Lower Canada), Nova Scotia, New Brunswick, Prince Edward Island. Images of this valuable fur-bearing mammal had been used as commercial and political emblems since early colonial times. But even here, the maple leaf sneaks into the picture – as a spray of leaves beneath the beaver's feet. The Three-Pence Beaver or Threepenny Beaver, as it quickly became known, was the world's first pictorial stamp, all previous postage stamps having had human portraits if they had any image on them at all. It remained in use as first-class postage until the late 1860s, making it the Dominion of Canada's first postage stamp.

The July 1853 issue of *The Illustrated Maple Leaf: A Canadian Magazine,* a monthly periodical aimed at older children, is an example of just how completely the emblem that originated in French Canada had been appropriated by English Canada by mid-century. The cover (not pictured here) displays about as many maple leaves as could fit on a single page. The leaves reappear on this contents page, along with a voyageur canoe running rapids, a dramatic rendering of Niagara Falls and a trusty beaver. But note the image of Britannia in the lower left and of Lord Nelson's *Victory* on the middle left. And undoubtedly the biggest draw of this inaugural issue was the first instalment of *Uncle Tom's Cabin,* by American writer Harriet Beecher Stowe. Among the magazine's regular Canadian contributors were Catharine Parr Trail, who wrote several serials, and her sister Susanna Moodie.

The "Old Flag" on Sir John A. Macdonald's famous election poster of 1891 is a Red Ensign, not a Union Jack, a subtle but definite message that the Tory prime minister was both a loyal British subject and a proud Canadian patriot. The "Old Leader" died shortly after his re-election, but his flag did not. In a letter to Macdonald's successor as prime minister, Charles Tupper, Governor General Lord Stanley wrote: "Though no actual order has ever been issued the Dominion government has encouraged, by precept and example, the use on all public buildings throughout the provinces, of the red ensign with the Canadian badge in the fly."

By comparison, when you think about the sugar maple leaf, you begin to understand how it won almost by default. Among our native trees, it and the oak carry perhaps the most ubiquitous and distinctive leaves, shapes instantly recognizable and easy to remember. But the maple leaf is more symmetrical than the oak and turns bright red, not dingy brown, each fall. It must have been one of the first and most vivid botanical images to become imprinted on the European brain.

The real plus for the maple leaf was its very lack of an established personality and its innocence of mythic or commercial associations. At a time when fierce tribal and religious loyalties repeatedly threatened the survival of the young dominion, anyone could look at the maple leaf and see an unassuming, neutral symbol that posed no threat to his or her identity or interests. Maybe the maple leaf emerged at the top of the symbolic heap because it was the perfect, perhaps the prototypical, Canadian compromise.

From 1867 to 1914 the story of Canada and its symbols is a tale of two nations – one French, one English – struggling to find a common ground for cohabitation. No better exhibit can be placed into evidence for this argument than the famous Tory election poster of 1891, created for Sir John A. Macdonald's last campaign. The poster's simple slogan speaks volumes: "The Old Flag. The Old Policy. The Old Leader." The old flag, surprisingly, is the Red Ensign, then having no official status in Canada but already managing to communicate a double loyalty, both to Great Britain and to Canada. (The Union Jack was then the only national flag.) But the poster was meant for English-Canadian eyes only. In French Quebec, Macdonald and his lieutenants campaigned as they always had: as protectors of the Catholic religion and of conservative social values.

Sir Wilfrid Laurier, who inherited from Macdonald the daunting task of keeping the country's centrifugal tendencies from tearing it apart, himself exhibited the national split personality. He was both a proud *Canadien* and a staunch British imperialist, convinced that French Canada's best hope of survival lay in remaining part of the British Empire. So great was his knowledge of British history that he could effortlessly call up examples from the Duke

The beautifully embossed leather case and decorative title page of *The Maple Leaf or Canadian Annual for 1847, a Literary Souvenir* provide two early examples of the appropriation of the maple leaf as an English-Canadian emblem. In the preface, the editor introduces the anthology thus: "When we formed the idea of offering to Canada a literary wreath, we determined that the only hands, which should weave the garland, should be those of her Children by birth or by adoption, and that no flowers, however lovely, should be twined with 'the maple leaf,' but those that had blossomed amidst her forests."

of Wellington's military exploits to bolster a political point to an English-Canadian audience. Without the extraordinary political skills of Canada's two true founding fathers, Macdonald and Laurier, the country we know today would not exist. They held it together long enough for a great war to provide real glue.

In the years leading up to the First World War, Canada's sense of self reached a point where a homegrown flag became a topic of general conversation – at least in anglophone areas. But the only uniquely Canadian alternative to the Union Jack, which since the union of Great Britain and Ireland in 1801 had included the cross of Saint Patrick, Ireland's patron saint, remained the Red Ensign.

The two sides in the flag debates of the 1960s told different stories about the status of the Canadian Red Ensign in the nineteenth century. One side scored technical points about the ensign's subsidiary status and lack of heraldic sanction; the other kept citing the many examples of its actual use. By definition, an ensign is a derivative of a national flag and thus subordinate to it – in this case a derivative of the Union Jack.

The British Red Ensign – with the jack in the upper left corner and no emblem in the fly – was first authorized for use by British merchant ships in 1707. The Canadian Red Ensign, which came officially into being by British Admiralty warrant in 1892 "to be used on board vessels registered in the Dominion," was therefore arguably a derivative of a derivative.

Yet the Canadian Red Ensign, which placed the unofficial shield of Canada (bearing the emblems of all the provinces) in the fly, must have been quite common already. As early as 1868, the government of the day began to fly it from atop the Victorian Tower, the predecessor of the Peace Tower. In 1891, Canada's governor general, Lord Stanley, could call it "the Flag which has come to be considered as the recognized Flag of the Dominion both afloat and ashore." Over the ensuing years the popular and unofficial use of the Canadian Red Ensign seems to have stayed well ahead of its official status. The Admiralty warrant of 1892 simply regularized a situation in which Canadian ships had for years been flying what the British considered an illegal flag. Not until 1924 did an order-in-council

THE BANNER WAVED by Lower Canadian Patriotes during the Rebellion of 1837 drew its main symbols from the natural world. The fish (haloed by a pine bough) is the *maskinonge*, or muskilunge, and the spray of leaves comes from a sugar maple The letters "C" and "J=Bte" can be read as "Canada for Saint Jean Baptiste." The flag's cloth, originally white, has yellowed with age, but its hand-painted devices have lasted well. This so-called Papineau flag was brandished by the rebels who followed Louis-Joseph Papineau in his quest for responsible government. Although the Patriotes enjoyed some initial military success, they were no match for the British regulars who defeated them at Saint-Charles and annihilated them at Saint-Eustache. In Upper Canada the rebellion was shorter-lived and even less successful, but it prompted Lord Durham's report, which recommended the union of Upper and Lower Canada, the first step toward Confederation.

À BAS LA TYRANNIE!

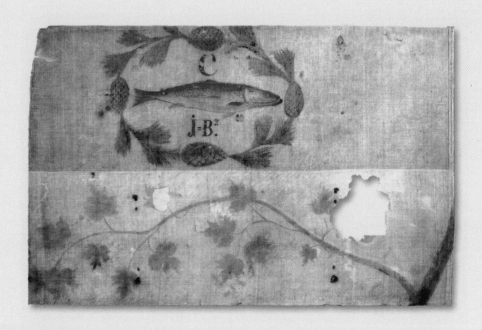

"A beautiful October day (Wednesday 25th) will long be remembered in the annals of Toronto; for then it was that we sent our brave boys to far-away Africa to fight the battles of Empire." So began the text in this pamphlet published in 1899 to honour the Toronto-area volunteers who had shipped to South Africa to join the Imperial brigades fighting the Boers. In battle, many of them would wear pith helmets emblazoned with a maple leaf. Several such helmets can be seen among the members of C Company of the Royal Canadian Regiment as they advance up the kopje across from the Boer camp at Paardeberg in December 1899 (*opposite*). Paardeberg was the first action in which Canadian troops took part and the battle that turned the military tide in Britain's favour.

permit the Canadian Red Ensign to be flown from federal government buildings abroad. In 1944 it earned the right "to be flown at all units of the Canadian Army serving with forces of other nations," but only in 1945 did an order-in-council sanction its use on government buildings on Canadian soil.

In the early years of the century, many English-speaking Canadians promoted the Red Ensign as an official national flag, continuing a quest that had begun while Sir John A. was still prime minister and one that he supported. But even among the ensign's most dedicated adherents, the maple leaf held its own. The Ontario and Quebec provincial emblems on the crowded shield in the Red Ensign's fly each consisted of the three-maple-leaf motif (Ontario's in green, Quebec's in gold). Even diehard adherents of the Union Jack, when arguing for the British flag as Canada's own, could not help but keep one eye on the native leaf.

But the most important campaign for the symbolic supremacy of the maple leaf was waged by Canadian soldiers at home and abroad. A staunch tradition dating from before Confederation included maple leaves as part of the identifying insignia of

Canadian regiments and on medals struck to reward military accomplishment. In 1859, for example, the Prince of Wales Royal Canadian Regiment (later the Leinster Regiment) was granted colours bearing maple leaves in each of its four corners – one of a number of early regiments that wore the maple leaf. The first specifically Canadian military medal, the General Service Medal of 1899, commemorated service in the Fenian Raids and the Red River Expedition of 1866–70. On one side sits a plump, grandmotherly Queen Victoria; on the other, a Canadian Red Ensign decorated with sprigs of maple leaves.

Many of the volunteers who sailed off to South Africa in 1899 to fight in the Boer War, this country's first foreign war (not counting the pre-Confederation War of 1812), wore a maple leaf on their helmets. According to one account, a Canadian who had been badly wounded at the Battle of Paardeburg placed his finger on his helmet's maple leaf and said, "If I die, it may help this live."

There is no question, however, that the maple leaf emblem came into its own in the First World War, along with the young

This General Service Badge (*above*) of the Royal Canadian Regiment was worn by its members who served in South Africa in 1899, further evidence of the early and widespread use of the maple leaf motif in the Canadian military.

2nd Canadian Mounted Rifles
First World War

7th Canadian Infantry Battalion
First World War

77th Canadian Infantry Battalion
First World War

63rd Canadian Infantry Battalion
First World War

FORGET ME NOT

84th Canadian Infantry Battalion
First World War

131st Westminster
First World War

Fort Garry Horse
Second World War

Queen's Own Rifles of Canada
Second World War

Almost every one of the metal badges affixed to this souvenir belt employs the maple leaf motif, often as its major design element. The belt is kept in a display case in the 109 Branch of the Royal Canadian Legion, in Gibsons, British Columbia. The badges range in date from the First World War through the Korean War. Presumably returning veterans from each overseas conflict contributed their personal souvenirs to an existing keepsake. The belt thus forms a sort of visual timeline while evoking the image of a column of soldiers marching off to war and, fewer in number, marching home. Here's how Brigadier-General Alexander Ross, who as a lieutenant-colonel commanded the 28th (North-West) Battalion at Vimy Ridge, described the impact of that epic battle: "It was Canada from Atlantic to Pacific on parade. I thought then … that in those few minutes I witnessed the birth of a nation."

Before the Battle of Amiens in early August 1918, a Canadian soldier (*above*) paints a maple leaf war crest on a tank – similar to the Mark V that was photographed passing the 8th Field Ambulance during the battle (*opposite*). But did any of the Canadians at Amiens fight under the Canadian Red Ensign? So far no concrete evidence to support this claim has been brought forward, though it was not unusual for Canadian soldiers in World War I to carry a souvenir ensign among their personal effects, a practice repeated in World War II. Through two world wars the maple leaf badge was the visible mark of a soldier's Canadian nationality.

country whose mark it had become. On the home front, that war divided Canada as dramatically as any episode in its history.

Prime Minister Robert Borden's 1917 decision to bring in conscription – the military draft – was a political winner in loyal English Canada and a vote killer in French Canada, where it meant forcing Quebec sons to serve under a British flag as part of an Imperial army (albeit in the defence of France). Once a conscripted soldier was sent overseas, it didn't matter whether his mother tongue was French or English, the maple leaf became his calling card.

When Lester Pearson reminded his Legion audience in Winnipeg of the metal maple leaf badges they had worn on their caps and collars during the First World War, he was not exaggerating. Among the hundreds of different badges identifying the battalions of the Canadian Corps, a badge without a maple leaf motif was rare. Most badges either used a single maple leaf as the organizing principle of their design or incorporated a wreath of maple leaves where a European badge would have employed a wreath of laurel leaves, the ancient Greek and Roman symbol of vic-

tory. As the men in the trenches idled away endless hours, one of their pastimes was to exchange and collect these badges, which they wore attached to a souvenir belt. Those who survived their wounds and made it through to the armistice brought their maple leaf talismans home with them.

Like Great Britain's other former colonies, Canada served in France as part of the British army. All the top commanders were British, and few of them knew a Canadian from an Australian from a South African from a New Zealander when the war began. That changed in April 1917, after the Canadian Corps, operating as a combined force for the first time, captured Vimy Ridge, a key strongpoint in the German defences in northeast France. The Canadian defensive gained more ground, captured more artillery pieces and took more prisoners than had any previous British action.

The troops owed their breakthrough to a potent combination of deference to authority and daring innovation. The Canadian Corps at Vimy seems to have been the first twentieth-century fighting force to fully adopt and successfully execute

THESE FOUR MOTHERS
GAVE TO THEIR COUNTRY
28 BRAVE SONS

The wounds of the First World War had not all healed before a second world conflict loomed. In the 1920s and 1930s, the annual Warriors Day Parade reminded Canadians how much they had lost in a conflict that was supposed "to end all wars." Few had lost more than these four bereaved mothers in a fabulously flag-decked automobile, who joined the parade of marching veterans sometime in the 1920s. In September 1939, after Canada declared war on Germany – an event delayed for several days because Prime Minister King was determined that Canada would enter the conflict independently from Great Britain – many young women enlisted in the three armed services. Here a recruiting booth for the Canadian Women's Army Corps *(below)* attracts the interest of a potential volunteer.

Lieutenant-Colonel Richard Malone (*on left*) helps mount the sign outside the editorial offices of the French edition of *The Maple Leaf* in recently occupied Caen, France, on July 11, 1944. The future editor-in-chief and publisher of *The Globe and Mail* had been tasked with establishing a daily newspaper for Canadian soldiers after they landed on European soil. The first number of the first edition was published in Naples on January 14, 1944. (The publication subsequently set up shop in the former Roman printing facilities of the socialist newspaper *Avanti!*) The first issues of the Western Front edition were produced while Caen was still under fire. According to one reminiscence, it was a rare day when none of the compositing machines or printing presses wasn't out of action.

progressive tactical thinking. Their commanding generals – Julian Byng and his Canadian subordinates Arthur Currie and artillery genius Andrew McNaughton – absorbed the best techniques wherever they found them. Then the Canadians added two crucial innovations of their own: they gave each soldier a map, and they figured out how to pinpoint and wipe out the enemy's artillery before the attack. At Vimy the Canadians made a major contribution to the invention of modern warfare.

After Vimy, so the story goes, a British officer one day approached a Canadian soldier and asked, "Are you a Canadian?" (No doubt he had noticed the fellow's maple leaf badge.) When answered in the affirmative, the officer replied, "I congratulate you upon it." Following the victory at Vimy Ridge this officer – and all his brothers – knew what a Canadian was.

Canada's conquering heroes carried home their new-found sense of a Canadian – as opposed to Imperial – identity, "a great surge of Canadian feeling which remains memorable in the hearts of those who wore the Maple Leaf," to quote just one of the countless reminiscences written by returning soldiers while the stench of battle was still fresh in memory. These men remembered the maple leaf as a badge of victory. It was seen likewise by the folks back home. A poem called "The Maple Leaves," written by Isabel Graham and published in the Toronto *Globe* on May 5, 1915, says it best.

> The maple leaves on Flanders' plain
> Fell in a hail of hellish rain.
> Their bright hues scattered o'er the sod,
> Far from their home, but near to God.
> The forest grieves,
> And softly sheathes
> Her dead, dead leaves.
>
> The maple leaves were heroes all;
> They rose at duty's clarion call,
> And grimly held the wavering line,
> Pouring out precious blood like wine.
> Now Glory weaves
> Immortal wreathes
> Of red, red leaves.

A country coming into awareness of itself seeks ways to express its uniqueness. And Parliament's initial attempt to give Canada its own official flag took place not

The Sopwith Dolphin bi-plane (*left*) belonged to No. 1 Squadron, Canadian Air Force, which wasn't formed until a week after the end of the First World War; like the Second World War mobile canteen (*below*) it used the familiar leaf to advertise its nationality. When Canadian troops advanced up the boot of Italy in the fall of 1943, they spent their precious furloughs at Maple Leaf City, a rest centre in Campobasso. One of its most popular hangouts, known as the Beaver Club, was a commandeered Fascist recreation centre.

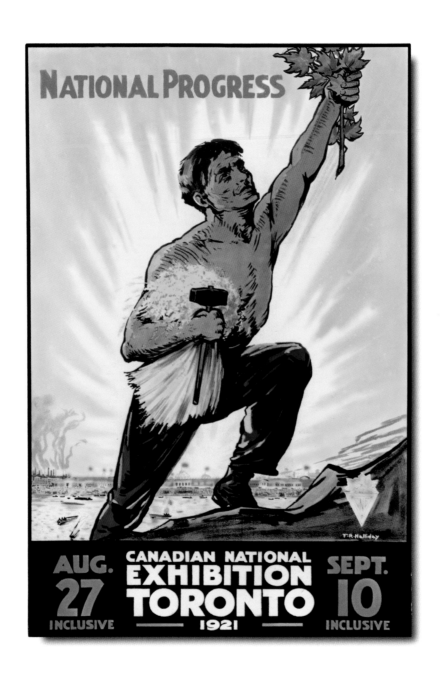

This CNE poster from 1921 *(opposite)*, with its image of a shirtless worker striving toward some invisible yet ideal world, could have come straight out of Joseph Stalin's propaganda workshops – except for the spray of bright red maple leaves the Canadian holds aloft, where a Soviet worker would have held a symbolic sickle. The same year, the International Stereotypers and Electrotypers Union of North America held its twentieth annual convention in Toronto. The Maple Leaf Convention program *(above)* was superbly printed, hand-tied and festooned with a frieze of maple leaves.

Canada's Myrtle Cook (*below far left*) wins her 100-metre heat at the 1928 games in Amsterdam, one of three Canadian women to make the final. In the final, however, Cook and teammate Ethel Smith were disqualified for false starts, leaving Bobby Rosenfeld to race to a silver second place in a disputed finish.

1182

long after the First World War's end. Predictably it came from the Liberal Party, then being painstakingly reassembled into a national electoral coalition by William Lyon Mackenzie King.

King makes for such a fascinating political figure in part because he combines two traditional and contradictory Canadian traits: a deep distaste for rocking the boat and a strong impulse toward social progress. In 1925, as his stewardship of Canada's first-ever minority government dwindled toward dissolution, King appointed a committee of civil servants to recommend a distinctive flag. His political antennae told him there was increasing public feeling for an end to the situation in which an unofficial flag – the Red Ensign – flew at Canadian embassies abroad but was not flown at home.

King's committee could stand on some recently achieved heraldic ground. In 1921, King George V had granted Canada an official coat of arms that superseded Canada's unofficial shield, by then badly overcrowded with all nine provincial emblems. He replaced it with a shield that deftly combined the emblems of England, Scotland, Ireland and France with the now indisputably

Canadian maple leaf. Simultaneously, he designated Canada's colours as red and white, both historically associated with England and France. Perhaps by accident, however, the artist who drew the official version of the arms copied the sprig of three green maple leaves that already appeared on the Ontario shield, an oversight corrected in 1957 by the government of John Diefenbaker. But despite growing public sentiment in the late 1920s in favour of doing something about a flag, the issue proved too hot for King to handle; he dissolved the committee before it could deliver its report.

Between the wars, the paradox of the growing popular use of the maple leaf emblem – especially in commerce and in sports – and the persistence of the Union Jack, mainly on the Canadian Red Ensign, grew more pronounced, as did confusion over which of Canada's "flags" one was supposed to fly. Some schools flew the ensign, some the jack; more often than not, the basis for choice seemed to be which flag was in good supply. Amidst all these mixed messages, the Canadian leaf persevered, especially in the arena of international sports, where, as long as most people could remember, every

By the 1900s, most Canadian athletes in international competition had adopted a maple leaf as their badge. A spray of examples: celebrated Onondaga marathoner Tom Longboat (*above left*); speedskater Frank Stack, who placed fourth at the Winter Olympics in 1932 (*above middle*); Billy Sherring, who won gold in the marathon at the 1906 Athens Olympics held to mark the tenth anniversary of the modern games (*above right*).

FROM CONFEDERATION ON, whenever Canadians sought to distinguish themselves from Britons, they flew a Canadianized version of the British red ensign, which had received official approval in 1892 in the form of a British Admiralty warrant permitting its use on Canadian merchant ships. Red ensigns bearing a shield quartered with the arms of the original four provinces (Nova Scotia, New Brunswick, Quebec and Ontario) appeared as early as 1868. As more provinces joined Canada, their emblems were added to the shield. By 1905, when Saskatchewan and Alberta became provinces, the shield bore as many as nine provincial badges.

There were no rules about the design of the shield or when and where the local flag could be flown and the outdated four-province

GROWING UP WITH THE ENSIGN

1921

version was still in wide use into the early 1920s. Starting in 1868, it flew on Parliament Hill, only to be replaced by the Union Jack in 1904 in a bout of post-Boer War Imperial patriotism.

During the twentieth century, the Canadian ensign slowly but surely edged toward official status. Whenever a Canadian flag was needed, it did the job – whether on a World War I recruiting poster or draped over the statue called Canada Mourning at the dramatic unveiling of the Vimy Memorial in 1936. And while the Union Jack remained Canada's national flag in peace and war, Canadian soldiers are known to have quietly carried their ensign into battle as early as Vimy Ridge. With the 1945 order-in-council that declared the Canadian ensign could be flown from "Federal government buildings within and without Canada," Canada's de facto flag appeared to be only steps away from official status.

Such was the situation in 1963, when Lester Pearson's Liberals came to power having promised that Canada would at last have its own distinctive national banner.

1868

1870

1873

1905

The evolution of the shield on the fly of the Canadian Red Ensign tells a tale of Canada's growth as a nation. (Note the varying treatments of the provincial emblems and the shield's frequent embellishment with a wreath of maple leaves, sometimes combined with laurel, plus royal crown and indigenous beaver.) The four-province shield of 1868 provided the template. Reading clockwise from the top left, we see the emblems of Ontario, Quebec, New Brunswick and Nova Scotia. Manitoba's bison joined these four in 1870, but there seems to have been no six-province version in response to British Columbia's arrival the following year. The westernmost province makes its appearance on the seven-province shield of 1873, along with a newly welcomed P.E.I. After 1905, Alberta and Saskatchewan crowd awkwardly onto the nine-province shield. It must have been a relief to flag makers when the king granted Canada a coat of arms in 1921. That year marked the birth of the ensign many Canadians still remember, wearing the new Canadian shield in the fly. (By an oversight, however, the maple leaves were originally coloured green instead of Canada's official red.)

The 1946 flag committee chose this variation on the Red Ensign to recommend to Parliament, but their choice never came to a vote in the House of Commons. Mackenzie King personally favoured the design, but he was far too cautious a politician to risk the political firestorm that would result.

Canadian team and almost all Canadian contestants had worn it as part of their uniforms.

At St. Louis, Missouri, in 1904 many of Canada's first Olympic athletes sported a nifty maple leaf insignia. At the first Winter Olympics – in Chamonix, France, in 1924 – a team of gifted amateurs called the Toronto Granites trounced all comers in the first official Olympic ice hockey competition while wearing a stylized maple leaf on their jerseys and sweater coats. In the 1920s and 1930s, wherever Canadian athletes went, their nationality could be instantly recognized by their maple leaf. Nor did it escape their notice that the leaf distinguished them far more successfully than the British-looking flag they carried at the opening and closing ceremonies.

The closest Canada came to getting its own flag before 1964 occurred soon after the Second World War, in another flush of national pride at Canada's major contribution to an Allied victory. Once again Canadians had fought with distinction. Once again they wore maple leaf cap and collar badges that clearly marked their nationality. And this time the maple leaf adorned every

ship at sea and every vehicle on land. As it had during the First World War, it served as the title of the armed forces newspaper, *The Maple Leaf.* But once again Canadian soldiers fought under a version of the British flag: until 1944 officially the Union Jack, thereafter officially the Red Ensign.

Back home after the war the flag question was referred to yet another parliamentary committee charged to "consider and report upon a suitable design" for "a distinctive national flag." The committee considered nearly three thousand designs and even put a selection of them on public display. Its report even made it to Parliament. But its choice – "the Canadian Red Ensign with a maple leaf in autumn gold colours in a bordered background of white replacing the Coat of Arms in the fly"– pleased no one, and it died on the order paper.

Yet with increasing urgency over the next two decades the flag question gained prominence. By the time John Diefenbaker became prime minister, the pressure to settle the argument was as great as ever. Just before Dief's government began to unravel in 1961, he promised to hold a federal-provincial conference to discuss the flag, a

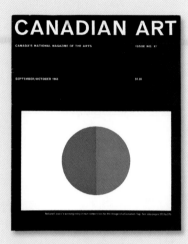

THE GREAT CANADIAN FLAG CONTEST

OVER THE ALMOST two decades between 1946 and 1964, the flag question continued to be asked and thousands of Canadians continued to answer with a bewildering array of proposals for a distinct national standard. Whenever someone held a flag contest – and there were a number during this period – the entries poured in. In September 1955, *Liberty*, "Canada's young family magazine," announced two prizes worth $1,000, one for adults (including a twenty-one-inch table model television set made by Canadian Marconi) and one for children (including an unlimited one-year pass to any of Canada's four hundred Famous Players theatres) for the best design. The flags bore "symbols ranging from a picture of a beaver driving a Cadillac, a Mountie on horseback, igloos, wigwams, lacrosse sticks, Indians in canoes, to a golden bull."

The editors of *Canadian Art* ran a rather more high-toned competition in 1963 when they teamed up with *Weekend Magazine.* The results reflected the modernist design mode of the day – which helps explain why so many of the finalists were so abstract, including the winner, which was featured on the magazine's cover (*above right*). "Our job," said Ted Bethune, "was to pick … the most distinctive flag which with simple, timeless, tasteful symbolism could eventually become known to the world as Canada and only Canada." According to Geoffrey Andrew, "The fact is we came into the business of nationalism too late to be content with symbols of a race and blood nationalism." And Guy Viau argued that Canada "should make it a point of honour to hoist a new flag as a symbol and a pledge of its unity and confidence in the future."

The painting by Rex Woods that appeared on the July 1954 cover of *Maclean's* wonderfully illustrates the ongoing, seemingly endless Canadian search for a national flag. Three suited bureaucrats hover over an artist at his drafting board. One points to the wall behind them, which is plastered with possible flag designs. All the while, the Red Ensign flies serenely outside the window, as if to say, "I don't know what all this fuss is about. Canada already has a flag, and I'm it!"

promise he never got the chance to fulfill.

So the baton was passed to Lester Pearson, who grasped it eagerly. Soon after Pearson's election in April 1963, the editors of *Weekend Magazine* and *Canadian Art* jointly sponsored a flag contest open only to professional artists and designers. The judges had to choose from among 783 entries, very few of which featured Union Jacks or fleurs-de-lys. None bore heraldic crowns or lions, and there was nary a beaver to be seen. A surprising number were completely abstract, but quite a few employed, singly or in all sorts of clever arrangements, a stylized maple leaf. The first prize of $2,000 went to an abstract design by Rolland Lavoie of Montreal. A stylized red maple leaf on a field of white by James Sanders of Toronto came second. That is where matters stood when Pearson rose in Parliament to propose his pennant.

By the time he did so, the maple leaf had grown far beyond its early status as a neutral symbol of indigenous origin to which each person could attach his or her own meaning, meanings that could be as different as loyalty to empire and faithfulness to the French fact. It had spread far and wide through popular culture with natural ease and had been adopted time and again for unofficial or semi-official use – whether as two words in a company's name or as an emblem embedded in its logo or to distinguish an athlete in international competition. It had been galvanized under fire, above all in the trenches of the First World War.

Before 1914 the maple leaf was a popular but still rather colourless symbol. After 1918 it was stained with blood and tinctured with victory; it could bear the symbolic weight of a nation. By 1964, when the Swinging Sixties swung at an ever quicker tempo, even those who held fast to the old symbols had to agree with Lester Pearson that the maple leaf had become "Canada's own and only Canada's."

"I don't think, young man, you're going to win this parliamentary struggle. It is not possible to legislate as a flag a design that has no significance and no tradition attached to it. To get a flag accepted, you have to have blood on it; you have to have waved it fighting somebody. That's how our flag became accepted. It was a badge of revolution; it was a badge of victory against our oppressors. You know what you ought to do, you really ought take your flag down to the American border ... and get some of your friends on the other side to take some shots at it, and if you can get somebody to be mildly wounded, that will make all the difference. It will be a hallowed emblem of your independence from the United States."

Irish President EAMON DE VALERA to Lester Pearson over dinner at Rideau Hall, spring 1964

CHAPTER THREE

The great debate

THE SUBDUED Mike Pearson who addressed the House of Commons on September 10, 1964, looked a different person from the man who had eloquently led off the Flag Debate on June 15, nearly three months before. John Diefenbaker's withering reply to the prime minister's opening speech had set off what was already one of the lengthiest and most rancorous episodes in Canadian parliamentary history, making a tattered rag of Pearson's overconfident prediction that the new flag might be flying by July 1. Thanks to the Tory filibuster, the debate had eaten up weeks of parliamentary time and brought the nation's business to a standstill while subjecting its elected representatives to the political equivalent of Chinese water torture. Everything that needed to be said on either side of the issue had been said back in June, yet the speeches continued. At one point the Liberal House leader, Jack Pickersgill, passed a note to his counterpart Gordon Churchill across the aisle: "If this performance is going to continue, please, please get a new speech writer who is not so boring and repetitive."

Outside the Commons, just as his opponents had predicted, the prime minister's quest to give Canada a distinctive flag seemed only to fan the flames of French-English animosity. In early October Queen Elizabeth II would be making an official visit to Quebec, with stops in Charlottetown, Quebec City and Ottawa, to mark the hundredth anniversary of the Charlottetown and Quebec Conferences of 1864 that had paved the way to Confederation. It did not take much imagination to predict trouble ahead.

Pearson's message to the House that day was simple and his tone conciliatory. He and his fellow party leaders had agreed – it had taken five meetings before they could come to terms – to refer the flag question to an all-party committee. The committee would have fifteen members: seven Liberals, five Conservatives, one New Democrat, two Créditistes. It would hold its meetings in camera and be required to report back to the House in six weeks. "I hope, Mr. Speaker," Pearson concluded, "the proposed committee will be successful in its work. It begins that work, I know, with the good will of all members on all sides of the House." And so it seemed. The next day the Canadian Press reported that with Pearson's words "the Chamber melted into an atmosphere of mutual good will."

Exhausted but jubilant Liberal members of Parliament celebrate the passage of the government's flag resolution in the wee hours of December 15, 1964. If the flag they're holding looks odd, it is. The leaf has thirteen points, a number that would be pared down to eleven before the design became final. From the portrait behind the celebrators, stern-looking Robert Borden, Tory prime minister from 1911 to 1920, appears to cast a disapproving eye on the proceedings.

A souvenir of Canada circa 1938. Although the sugar maple doesn't grow anywhere near the Rockies, here its leaf helps say western Canada. The postcard itself provides a nice visual summary of the symbols that faced off during the debate of 1964: the Union Jack and the Red Ensign on one side of the flag divide, the maple leaf and other homegrown emblems, like this iconic Mountie, on the other. The equivalent postcard could be purchased today, sans Anglo references.

ROYAL CANADIAN MOUNTED POLICE, CANADA

Pearson had counted on public opinion to force the Conservatives to relent and let the flag resolution come to a vote. He had not counted on Diefenbaker's staying power. Now he had been forced to beat a strategic retreat. Referring the issue to a committee was far better than the alternatives – invoking closure (a rule that permits the government to end a debate arbitrarily by a majority vote) or withdrawing the flag resolution altogether – but would it work? Twice before, in 1925 and 1945–46, the flag question had been handed to a committee. Twice before the committee had been derailed by tribal passions and party politics. And the odds seemed heavily stacked against securing the majority needed to give sufficient weight to the committee's recommendation. More likely it would end in a stalemate. And if the fifteen MPs failed to come up with a design that could be sold to the House and to the country, Pearson's noble flag initiative would almost certainly fall into ruins. No doubt Diefenbaker hoped for precisely this outcome, which would so weaken the government that he would be able to force an election.

Maybe Pearson was being foolhardy.

Maybe he figured he had nothing to lose. Or maybe he knew exactly what he was doing. The veteran of countless diplomatic negotiations must have realized by now that his personal choice – the three red leaves flanked by two blue bars – would never fly. He certainly understood that the Red Ensign was unacceptable to many Canadians and most French-speaking Canadians, that the winning compromise would be neither of these. And he would let that compromise be crafted by a committee. With this decision, Lester Bowles Pearson shows up in a most appealing light, as a man prepared to do the right thing even if it meant risking the most embarrassing failure of his young prime ministership. The right thing also happened to be the most parliamentary thing. He would let a group of elected members choose their country's flag.

The committee met for the first time a week later, on September 17, in Committee Room 356S, on the third floor of the Senate side of the Centre Block. Except for this first administrative meeting, all their sessions would be held in camera. The fourteen men and one woman found

During the endless August of 1964, as the Flag Debate dragged on in the House of Commons and parliamentary politeness wilted in the summer heat, John Diefenbaker seemed inexhaustible in his opposition to the Pearson Pennant. Here he emerges to face the daily scrum of reporters looking fresh as a maple bud in spring.

Herman Batten (*at left*), chair of the 1964 Flag Committee, was by all accounts a superb choice. Members from all parties gave him credit for grace under pressure. And by the end of their six weeks together, the fifteen MPs must have felt as if they were living inside a flag-decked pressure cooker. (Vice-Chair Théogène Ricard sits beside Batten.)

themselves in a cocoon whose walls were padded with maroon carpeting and whose table and chairs were of polished mahogany. They represented different parties, every region of the country and both official languages. Given the demographics of the 1960s House of Commons, they represented the country about as well as could be expected, as a simple listing of their names and constituencies confirms:

- Herman Batten, Liberal, Humber-St. George's (Newfoundland)
- Léo Cadieux, Liberal, Terrebonne (Quebec)
- Grant Deachman, Liberal, Vancouver Quadra (British Columbia)
- Jean-Eudes Dubé, Liberal, Restigouche-Madawaska (New Brunswick)
- Hugh John Flemming, Conservative Victoria-Carleton (New Brunswick)
- Margaret McTavish Konantz, Liberal, Winnipeg South (Manitoba)
- Raymond Langlois, Créditiste, Mégantic (Quebec)
- Marcel Lessard, Créditiste, Lac-Saint-Jean (Quebec)
- Joseph Macaluso, Liberal, Hamilton West (Ontario)

- John Ross Matheson, Liberal, Leeds (Ontario)
- Jay Waldo Monteith, Conservative, Perth (Ontario)
- David P. Pugh, Conservative, Okanagan Boundary (British Columbia)
- Reynold Rapp, Conservative, Humboldt-Melfort Tisdale (Saskatchewan)
- J. H. Théogène Ricard, Conservative, St-Hyacinthe- Bagot (Quebec)
- Reid Scott, NDP, Danforth (Toronto, Ontario)

From the perspective of the early twenty-first century, it's easy to criticize the narrowness of the committee's ethnic and religious makeup. With the exception of Reynold Rapp, an ethnic German from the Russian Crimea, whom Matheson described as "now more British than the British," all were Canadian-born, and the fourteen who professed a religious affiliation were all Christians. But the committee's profile reflected the House of Commons as a whole. For example, even if the party leaders had wanted to include a representative of Canada's Native peoples, there was none to be found in either government or opposition ranks. (Leonard Marchand, Canada's first

THANKS TO SCHULZ

Aboriginal cabinet minister, would not be elected until 1968.) Still, by 1964 more than 25 percent of Canadians traced their origins to neither France nor the British Isles, and that proportion was steadily rising. Yet parliamentary democracy depends on the principle that each freely elected representative must attempt to represent the interests of all his or her constituents. In the case of the 1964 Flag Committee, this principle would be put to the highest test.

Herman Batten, who was as "solid as English oak," in Matheson's estimation, accepted the chair when Matheson declined. As the MP most closely associated with Pearson and his pennant, the member from Leeds figured he'd be more effective at brokering a compromise from the sidelines. By all accounts, Batten did an admirable job of keeping the committee pressure cooker from blowing. It helped, Matheson would recall, to have Margaret Konantz's civilizing presence in the room.

The committee started out on a conciliatory note, with everyone quite conscious of the importance of their task. And despite the later Liberal tendency to dismiss the Tories as little more than Diefenbaker's

Canadian editorial cartoonists have seldom had as much fun as they had during the Flag Debate. Pearson and Diefenbaker were both made for caricature, and the political circus that accompanied the debate required little comic exaggeration.

Here the *Toronto Telegram*'s John Collins pays homage to Charles Schulz by rendering both the Liberal and Tory leaders as versions of Linus, with Linus's ever-present blanket replaced by each man's flag of comfort.

The Flag Committee began its deliberations with a sense of historical mission and in a spirit of cooperation. It wouldn't last. Before its in camera sessions grew heated, however, the chairman allowed the press in to take some photographs. (*Left to right*) Waldo Monteith, Léo Cadieux, Reynold Rapp, John Matheson, Raymond Langlois, Reid Scott, Joseph Macaluso, Hugh John Fleming, David Pugh, Margaret Konantz, Marcel Lessard, Grant Deachman, Jean-Eudes Dubé, Maxine Guitard (clerk of the committee), Herman Batten, Théogène Ricard.

The committee's first witness, Colonel Archer Fortescue Duguid, told its members that the Canadian Red Ensign was indistinguishable from the flag of Bermuda (*below*). Later in his testimony Duguid argued forcefully against the adoption of a one-maple-leaf flag: "A single leaf is very, very general; it is not exclusive to the Government of the Dominion of Canada. That is why it is perfectly all right for vendors of anything, be it gasoline or bacon; they have a perfect right if they wish to use one maple leaf and they do. The use of a single maple leaf by the Dominion of Canada would not be sufficiently distinctive." Duguid would later publicly criticize the committee's final choice.

hand-picked puppets, a diary that Waldo Monteith kept during the life of the committee suggests he and his colleagues started out as eager as anyone to come up with an acceptable compromise.

Monteith's entry for the second meeting, held on the afternoon of September 21, concludes on a hopeful note: "The final impression was that everybody was speaking quite candidly, and to be quite honest if anybody was holding their hand somewhat and not giving an indication of what they would not accept it was Flemming, Rapp and Monteith. The Chairman and the Vice-Chairman [Théogène Ricard] did not express their views." The former Diefenbaker cabinet minister annotated the diary typescript after the committee had delivered its report. Following the entry just quoted, he wrote in pen, "How wrong I was!"

The fifteen MPs had no dearth of designs to choose from. In addition to the roughly two thousand submitted directly to the committee, another thirty-nine hundred had to be waded through and weeded out. These included designs considered by the parliamentary committee of 1946. The weeding was done by a steering committee consisting of the committee chair (Batten) and vice-chair (Ricard), Grant Deachman, Waldo Monteith and Reid Scott. Soon the committee room walls were plastered with possibilities. When wall space ran out, committee members began hanging their favourites from the ceiling. One press report characterized the effect of hundreds of flag designs in "all colour combinations and motifs" as a "blinding sight."

Many of these flags bore Union Jacks and fleurs-de-lys. Quite a few featured a beaver, including one wearing a Mountie hat; another one showed an adult beaver encircled by ten smaller ones (Canada and its provinces). Other wild creatures included Canada geese, grizzly bears, moose, salmon, bison, caribou. The North Star was a popular emblem, as was the cross. Several designs included Aboriginal symbols. And one, submitted by the self-proclaimed "Society for the Suppression of Blue Lines" of Toronto, consisted of "crossed red hockey sticks rampant" and a single hockey puck.

But the overwhelming majority of the flags that made it onto the committee room walls featured a maple leaf, with or without competing emblems. The leaf

Artist A.Y. Jackson not only testified before the committee, he submitted two different flag designs, the single-leaf version *(below)* and the three-red-leaf version *(right).* To him the wavy blue bars represented the rivers of Canada, the historic means by which the country was opened up.

These nineteen flag designs from among the almost six thousand considered by the 1964 Flag Committee exhibit the prevalence of the maple leaf emblem among a wide variety of Canadian motifs.

A. F. MacDonald
H. Victor Wells
Alain J. Esariste

George Bist
Germain Tremblay
Artist Unknown
Artist Unknown

Osy-Mandias Pauling
T. G. A. Henstridge
Valentine A. McInnes
Arnold Weir

Adam Casson
Artist Unknown
J. C. Prefontaine
Alma Diebolt

W. Howard Ellis
Germain Tremblay
Valentine A. McInnes
J. C. Prefontaine

Seventy-one years before the 1964 Flag Committee began its deliberations, one of Canada's most famous nation-builders made public his rather forward-looking proposal for a distinctive Canadian flag. Sandford Fleming's "meteor flag of the Dominion" substituted a seven-pointed North Star for the usual Canadian shield on the fly of the already popular Red Ensign. One point stood for each of the seven provinces. In defence of his choice, Fleming made short work of the usual candidates. The beaver: "There are other members of the same natural order (Rodentia), such as rats and mice, not less active and industrious than the beaver, and for this quality alone no one would dream of selecting one of these vermin for our national emblem." The maple leaf: "If a single green leaf be plucked it shrivels in a few hours … In no form has the maple leaf the quality of the endurance which we desire."

came singly, or as two or three conjoined, or in the form of a wreath or garland. In some versions the leaves were organized like the stars in the Stars and Stripes. Others tried out all sorts of modifications on the Pearson design, including a single red leaf between blue bars. The Group of Seven's A.J. Casson submitted a proposal; the Group's A.Y. Jackson submitted two.

On September 23, the committee heard its first witness, Colonel Archer Fortescue Duguid, who gave the members a stern lesson in Canadian heraldry and annoyed the Tories on the committee by tartly dismissing the Red Ensign as virtually indistinguishable from the flag of Bermuda, or for that matter, from its progenitor, the ensign of the British merchant marine. Time and again Duguid returned to the simple heraldic solution: an argent (white) field charged with three red (gules) maple leaves was the correct Canadian symbol and the only logical choice.

The testimony of the remaining eleven witnesses ranged from the sublime to the silly. On the sublime end of the scale sat historian Arthur Lower, the distinguished author of *Colony to Nation*, who provided some sobering reflections on the health of the Canadian body politic and wondered aloud whether Canada would ever rise above its divisions to become a truly united country. Ominously, he compared the temper of the times to the mood in the United States in the years before the Civil War. Lower didn't come right out and say he favoured a maple leaf flag, but he argued persuasively against choosing a patchwork of British and French symbols: "The only thing that will replace the old sentiments is a powerful new sentiment, a sentiment for the country as a whole."

At the most puzzling point on the continuum sat Professor Marcel Trudel from Université Laval, who argued forcefully for a position that could have been scripted by John Diefenbaker. "I am convinced, for my part, that any flag, if it is to be truly significant, must contain or represent the symbols of the nation or nations which contributed to establishing the country," he declared, before deriding the maple leaf as of "no historic significance. It makes no difference whether the flag has three leaves or one leaf." The silliest episode in the testimony likely came when Group of Seven

This simple three-leaf design on a white background most pleased heraldic purists such as Colonel Duguid and his disciple John Matheson. Canada's colours were red and white, Duguid reminded the committee, and its official emblem was three red maple leaves on a single stem. But where Duguid was adamant, Matheson was willing to compromise.

In its determination to consider all reasonable possibilities, the 1964 Flag Committee reduced the thousands of designs submitted to the government by Canadians since the end of the Second World War down to a visual pool of a few hundred. It is interesting to speculate how they decided which designs made this first cut. The selection reproduced here, now held at Canada's National Archives, ranges from the refined to the jejune but indicates the tidal wave of creative energy the flag question released.

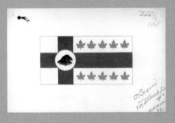

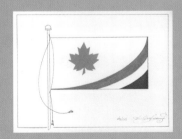

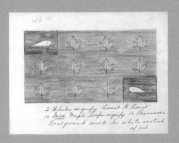

In April 1959, John Heysel crossed the country in his crusade for a new flag. Heysel seems to have been attached to no organization or interest group. He just wanted the flag question settled. But various organizations were also active in the quest. One of these was the Native Sons of Canada, which produced a pamphlet in the early 1960s displaying all sorts of possible Canadian flags. "For years Canadians have argued about whether we should have a distinctive national flag ... and there seems to be pretty general agreement that a Canadian flag is not only desirable but essential."

icon A.Y. Jackson (he was accompanied by art collector Robert McMichael) ended up debating the aesthetics of specific designs with various committee members, none of whom appeared to have the faintest knowledge of graphic art. The distinguished painter responded intelligently and politely nonetheless.

The witnesses included three historians (Lower, Trudel and Stewart McNutt from the University of New Brunswick) and a professor of political economy from the University of Toronto (Donald MacGregor), whose sole qualification seems to have been that flags were his hobby. Historian Donald Creighton had been invited but was either unable or unwilling to testify. Alan Beddoe added his heraldic point of view to Colonel Duguid's. Howard Measures, the government's director of protocol, and Alan Winship, from the Privy Council Office, provided lessons in flag etiquette and the niceties of passing and promulgating flag legislation.

On Thursday, October 8, the committee met for its twentieth and twenty-first sessions. They had by now heard most of the witnesses. They had argued strenuously

back and forth. But they seemed no closer to reaching an acceptable compromise. The next day, as many of them headed home to their constituencies for the weekend, they must have wondered whether they were wasting their time.

Any who tuned in to the CBC news on the following Saturday learned that their job had just become a good deal more urgent. The week-long visit of the Queen of Canada, which had commenced on October 6 in Charlottetown, had reached its climax. On that chilly grey Saturday morning, Premier Jean Lesage appeared visibly agitated as he awaited the Queen's arrival at Wolfe's Cove, Quebec, off which the royal yacht *Britannia* lay at anchor. Under the circumstances, the spot where General James Wolfe and the British forces had landed before climbing the cliffs to surprise the French and fight the Battle of the Plains of Abraham in 1759 seemed a spectacularly poor choice for the royal point of entry. The premier, who had been receiving separatist kidnapping threats for months and sloughed them off, had the previous day received an anonymous threat that his youngest son, Raymond, would be

Governor General Georges Vanier, a founding officer of the famous Van Doo regiment, escorts Queen Elizabeth II during her visit to the Quebec Citadel in October 1964. The Queen had come to pay her respects to the regiment of which she was an honorary colonel and to inaugurate a memorial to its war dead. While she reviewed the troops, about seventy-five separatist protesters managed to scale one of the Citadel walls, atop which they sat and sang and chanted.

kidnapped if the British queen was allowed to set foot on Quebec soil. He hadn't slept at all the previous night.

The threats helped explain the oppressive security as the royal couple disembarked to the accompaniment of a twenty-one-gun salute fired from the Quebec Citadel on the heights above. Premier Lesage was gracious in his welcoming remarks, but reporters who'd received a copy in advance knew he had cut them drastically short; others noted that his hands trembled as he spoke. Phalanxes of Mounties shielded the Queen from contact with the few of her loyal Quebec subjects who had braved the cordon sanitaire in hopes of catching a glimpse of their sovereign.

The year to date had been a relatively quiet one on the separatist front, devoid of exploding mailboxes or other acts of violence. But the dream of some sort of Quebec independence, either within or without Canada, was gaining a hold on more and more of Quebec's politicians and opinion-makers, among them a powerful minister in the Lesage government named René Lévesque.

The trouble in Quebec City began early that Saturday and dogged the Queen at every pause in her royal progress. As she addressed the Quebec legislature in her excellent French, a small crowd of separatist protesters demonstrated peacefully on the grounds outside. While she described Canada as "a meeting-place of two great civilizations, each contributing its own genius and dignity," the demonstrators shouted "Le Québec aux Québécois." When she spoke of the "irreplaceable role and special destiny of French Canada," the police outside the legislature charged the protesters and began making arrests.

That evening a lavish state dinner was held at the Château Frontenac. Inside the Château a radiant young queen dazzled the guests with "the most stunning ensemble of her present visit to Canada," according to the Montreal *Gazette*: a cinnamon silk tulle dress with a full skirt and a diamond tiara interlaced with opals and large pearls. Outside, a small contingent of young demonstrators, mostly students, were heading home after their long day of largely peaceful protest when hundreds of police brandishing riot sticks charged. The protesters panicked and a number were injured as they tried to escape – as were

Elsewhere the protests did not turn out so peacefully. On several occasions during the day, truncheon-wielding Quebec City police attacked groups of mostly student protesters, injuring several and arresting many. (Here police struggle with a student they've taken into custody outside the Quebec legislature, while inside Queen Elizabeth is giving her remarks to the assembled legislators.) The respected French-language newspaper *Le Devoir* was as critical as any in the country when it condemned police for "un excès incompréhensible de rudesse et de zèle," while noting that the Queen's speech was "lucide et positif" in its support for constitutional reform.

Two first-day covers (special envelopes that can be sent with a stamp on its first day of issue): the Canadian War Effort issue of 1942 and an issue marking the tenth anniversary of Queen Elizabeth's accession to the throne in 1952. The two covers suggest the range of treatments possible for an emblematic maple leaf. The wartime issue reproduces the ornate form of the silver maple. The 1962 issue employs a sugar maple leaf.

several reporters. By the time the royal visitors flew off to Ottawa the next morning, the whole world had heard of what came to be known as "le samedi de la matraque" (Truncheon Saturday).

Perhaps the Queen's visit had concentrated a few minds when the members of the Flag Committee reconvened on the afternoon of Tuesday, October 13. None of them could now doubt the seriousness of Canada's current unity crisis or the importance of their deliberations. But a successful result appeared as distant as ever. This may explain why John Matheson made a last-ditch attempt to bring the factions together by brokering a compromise with his friend and adversary Waldo Monteith.

About 11:15 pm on Thursday, October 15, Monteith was watching the news in his Ottawa apartment when the phone rang. It was Matheson, wondering if he and Alan Beddoe could drop over for a late-night visit. (Beddoe had been serving as the committee's chief designer and resource on heraldry, rendering various design ideas into graphic form for the group's consideration.) Monteith agreed. His diary reports that they brought with them "a design of

the three maple leaves with the Jack in one corner and the fleur-de-lys in another. I intimated that in my opinion there was too much white in the background and that it would not really be a good flag, but then Beddoe undertook to make some alterations and the three of us would discuss the matter later. It was agreed that no mention, for the time being, would be made to the other Committee members of our meeting. Matheson undertook that if I would accept some similar design he would sell it to his Party members."

Was Matheson serious? Could he have sold such a compromise to the other Liberals on the committee, let alone the two Quebec Créditistes or the NDP's Reid Scott? Highly unlikely. But the committee's report was due in less than two weeks, and a good negotiator knows that unless you keep both sides talking, no deal is possible.

Beddoe met with Monteith a second time on Sunday night, when they went over the different mock-ups the artist had been working on. "We spent 3/4 hour discussing these 12 designs," Beddoe confided to his diary, "and he told me that when John and I went to see him last Thurs. night after

The *Toronto Telegram's* Andy Donato captured the political conundrum perfectly in his cartoon depicting the four federal party leaders (*left to right*, Pearson, Diefenbaker, Douglas, Caouette) holding a flag that might aptly be described as an ensign defaced in every quarter.

THE FINAL FIFTEEN

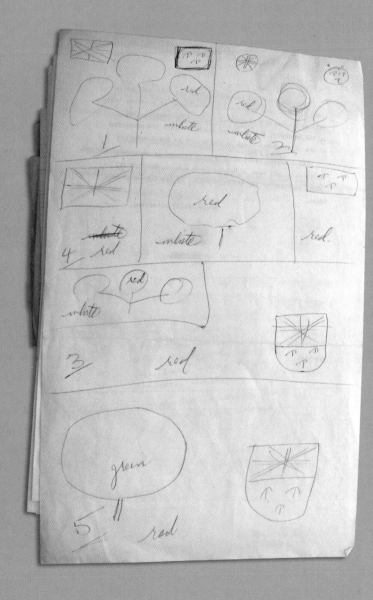

SADLY, much of the documentary evidence that might shed light on the final deliberations of the Flag Committee has disappeared, including most of Alan Beddoe's careful colour mock-ups of the fifteen final designs that competed with each other on the day of decision, October 22, 1964. Apart from the semi-finalists that emerged from each group of five and then faced off in the decisive round of voting, we can only guess what these other flags looked like – except for those in Group C, the last refuge for designs bearing emblems of other countries (the Union Jack, the fleur-de-lys). This is because Waldo Monteith, the lead Tory on the committee, sketched the five contestants in Group C on a loose sheet of paper that ended up in the Monteith collection preserved at Library and Archives Canada (LAC). Though Monteith was no draftsman, his sketches are clear enough. (The flag that moved forward to the final round is the third sketch of the sequence, even though he has labelled it with the numeral 4.) An exhaustive search of the LAC holdings has found only a handful of the missing final designs, but the rest may yet turn up.

the meeting, it was the first ray of hope he had seen for a solution to the impasse." Of the same meeting, Monteith reports that Beddoe presented him with "some 10 or 12 different designs incorporating the Union Jack and the fleur-de-lys in various combinations." Beddoe and Matheson met with Monteith once more on Monday afternoon to settle on several acceptable compromises that Beddoe would show to the committee the following afternoon. The next morning Beddoe called Monteith to tell him that "he had been talking to London and the Office of the Garter King-of-Arms [the head of the Royal College of Arms] and there was nothing wrong heraldically speaking with the Fleur-de-Lys being imposed on the Union Jack."

Here the documentary trail of Matheson's back-channel diplomacy goes cold. The designs he and Beddoe had developed for Monteith didn't get very far with the committee. But one of them became the compromise choice of the Anglo Tories. Reid Scott remembers this one being jokingly referred to as "Dief's abomination." Unaware of Matheson and Beddoe's involvement, he and most of his non-Tory

colleagues assumed Monteith was taking his orders directly from the Chief. The sessions grew more fractious as the day of decision loomed. Monteith's diary telegraphs the worsening weather. At the head of his entry for Tuesday morning, October 21, the day before the committee was due to vote, he writes, "STORMIEST MEETING YET!" Did he even notice the latest design that had been added to the committee room's flag wallpaper?

Success has many fathers, or so the saying goes. And many people have since taken credit for coming up with the red-white-red, single-maple-leaf design. Reid Scott claims that he had been advocating something like it all along; he was on record in the House and in the press as wanting a single leaf between Pearson's two blue bars. Several one-leaf designs were considered by the committee, but the one that ultimately occupied the foreground did not enter the lists until John Matheson suddenly remembered George Stanley's letter.

Lieutenant-Colonel George F.G. Stanley, who then held the position of dean of arts at Royal Military College in Kingston, Ontario, was a distinguished historian with

The flag of the Royal Military College in Kingston, Ontario, inspired George Stanley's one-leaf-flag idea, which played a key role in the committee's ultimate decision. Had Stanley been able to testify before the increasingly fractious group of MPs, however, he would probably have been perceived as Matheson's man and his suggestion dismissed.

George Stanley sketched these two designs in red pencil on the letter he sent to John Matheson on March 23, 1964. After Canada's national flag became law, Stanley's letter went missing; it wasn't rediscovered until 2000 by archivist Glenn Wright, who found it lodged among Alan Beddoe's papers at the National Archives. Presumably, when Matheson asked Beddoe to mock up a single-leaf design based on Stanley's idea, he gave Beddoe Stanley's letter. Matheson never thought to ask for its return.

GEORGE STANLEY, FLAG ARTIST

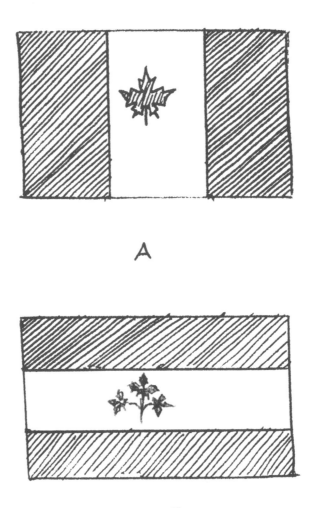

A

B

> "The single leaf has the virtue of simplicity; it emphasizes the distinctive Canadian symbol; and suggests the idea of loyalty to a single country."

GEORGE F.G. STANLEY, dean of arts, Royal Military College of Canada, March 23, 1964

an unusual perspective on the flag issue. At RMC he helped educate cadets from both French and English Canada. He was a veteran of the Second World War and the author of the first sympathetic biography of Louis Riel written by an English Canadian. For these reasons, as well as the fact that John Matheson counted Stanley as a friend, he had wanted him to testify before the committee. This could not be arranged.

However, back on March 23, at Matheson's request, Stanley had written him a memorandum outlining the historical and heraldic background of the various symbols under consideration and summarizing what the RMC historian considered to be the "principles to be followed in the selection of a Canadian flag":

(a) simplicity – it should be clean cut and not cluttered.

(b) easily recognizable.

(c) use traditional colours and traditional emblems.

(d) serve as a rallying symbol and hence be a unifying force.

Stanley's letter went on to make a very clear case for a flag that contained only the "traditional colours now associated with Canada," which are red and white, and for its central symbol to be "the traditional heraldic device or emblem of Canada," which is the maple leaf. Then he drew two possible designs for red-and-white maple leaf flags. One consisted of two horizontal red bars above and below a horizontal white bar charged with three red maple leaves; the other, two vertical red bars flanking a white bar of equal width charged with a single stylized maple leaf. In expressing his support for the single-leaf version, Stanley noted that it was very close in concept to the flag of the Royal Military College, "the basic difference being the inclusion of the RMC crest (armed fist) in the white third."

The one-leaf design with the vertical red bars had an elegant simplicity that pleased Matheson. Here, he thought, was a compromise that a majority of the committee members might accept, a maple leaf flag that was definitely not the Pearson Pennant. For Matheson, it meant giving up any lingering hope he held of getting a flag that was precisely correct in heraldic terms. But as Stanley had pointed out in the letter's closing paragraph, "a flag is not a coat of arms, but a heraldic device in its simplest and most primitive form." Matheson reminded himself that there was ample precedent for the single maple leaf, from the uniforms worn by Canadian athletes at the 1904 Olympic Games to the "single leaf carved in stone at the head of each overseas grave for Canada's fallen dead." At about the time that his back-channel negotiations with Monteith faded out, he instructed Beddoe to draft a fully realized version of Stanley's idea, then without fanfare added it to all the others on the committee room walls.

In practical political terms, Reid Scott and his two Créditiste colleagues from Quebec, Raymond Langlois and Marcel Lessard, held the committee's swing votes. If they sided with the five Tories, Monteith would have a bare majority of eight to six. If they voted with the six Liberals, the majority would be nine to five. (The chair voted only to break a tie.) The NDPer and his Créditiste colleagues all favoured a single leaf, while Scott believed that Matheson was still stuck on the three-leaf flag. He did not know that Pearson's close ally had never liked those heraldically incorrect blue bars.

Among the thousands of designs proposed for the new Canadian flag in 1964, this one takes the cake as a Canadian compromise. It's a Quebec flag in which the fleur-de-lys in the canton has been replaced with a Union Jack.

Following one of the last sessions before the vote, Scott loitered in the committee room to chat with Matheson. When they were alone, the Toronto New Democrat offered the opinion that the three-leaf design hadn't a hope of winning. Robert McKeown's account of the scene, published in *Weekend Magazine* a few weeks after the events, is probably as close to the truth as any.

"Is there anything else you would accept?" Scott asked.

They went over the various flags left on the wall. Only the one-leaf flag originally suggested by Dr. Stanley caused Matheson to demur. "Certainly it has a lot that's right about it," he said.

"Would you vote for it?" Scott asked.

"You're pressing me hard," said Matheson. "You know how committed I am to the other one."

"Will you vote for it?" Scott insisted. "If you do I think the others will."

Matheson indicated that he might bring himself to vote for the red-white-red design.

"I realized," he said later, "that it was not just a compromise. It was completely acceptable on its own behalf."

Grant Deachman, who was the committee member in charge of Liberal strategy, was immediately brought into the loop. His only hesitation was whether Pearson would give up his three-leaf pennant. So he and Matheson and Joe Macaluso went to see their boss. The prime minister immediately gave his okay. Then Deachman and Scott worked out a strategy that would ensure its selection.

Shortly after 10:30 a.m. on October 22, the Flag Committee convened for its thirty-fifth session. The members were worn out and under extreme pressure. The Tories reasonably assumed that no "substantial majority" for any one design would be possible. Waldo Monteith moved one last time that the flag question be put to a national plebiscite, his party's public position since the Flag Debate began. The motion was voted down along strict party lines, five for, nine against. The way was now clear for voting on the fifteen finalists, which had been cannily grouped into three categories: Group A – designs incorporating the three-maple-leaf emblem; Group B – designs featuring a single maple leaf; Group C – designs containing "symbols of other countries" (the Union Jack and/or the fleur-de-lys).

After a mind-numbing series of secret ballots, the choices were finally narrowed down to one in each category. The finalist from Group A was – no surprise – the blue-barred, three-red-leaf design originally favoured by Pearson, which the Tories believed the Liberals were still committed to; from Group B the committee chose the single-leaf flag derived from the suggestion made by George Stanley; from Group C it singled out a crowded red-and-white flag with the Union Jack in the top left-hand corner, three fleurs-de-lys in the fly and a single maple leaf in the centre.

Which of the three semi-finalists would survive the simple yes/no vote and reach the finals? The Pearson flag, the contestant from Group A, barely stayed in the running, eight votes to six. The single leaf from Group B received thirteen votes to one, suddenly emerging as the favourite. The vote on the contestant from Group C wasn't even close: Monteith's carefully crafted compromise lost by nine votes to five. A sudden-death final secret ballot would decide between the three-leaf and the one-leaf flags.

At the end of six gruel-
ling weeks, the Flag Com-
mittee's choices came
down to three designs,
each featuring a stylized
red sugar maple leaf on
a white background. But
to the bleary eyes of the
committee members,
the three finalists com-
municated three very
different messages. The
Group A finalist, a.k.a.
the Pearson Pennant,
looked to the Opposition
members like a Liberal
Party flag. As such, it didn't
stand a chance of emer-
ging as the winner.

GROUP A FINALIST

A.Y. Jackson derided the stylized maple leaf created by Alan Beddoe as looking like it was "cut out of leather," adding that "a stylized maple leaf is not a maple leaf at all." But Beddoe's one-leaf idea communicated simply and powerfully, easily emerging as the finalist in Group B. With refinements, this is the design that ultimately became Canada's national flag.

If the Group C finalist had won the day, it would have generated endless jokes about how Canada's flag was designed by a committee. Beddoe's compromise represents a failed effort to please everybody that succeeded in pleasing only the Tories on the Flag Committee, with the possible exception of Québécois Tory MP Théogène Ricard, who ultimately voted for the Maple Leaf flag.

GROUP C FINALIST

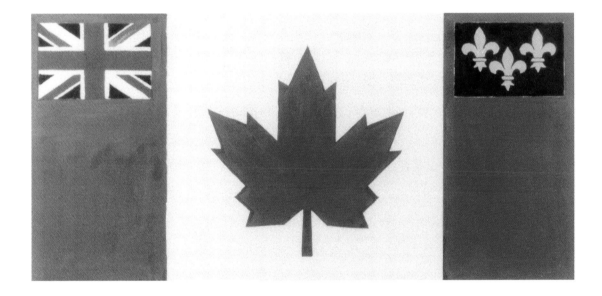

When the winning flag design was leaked before the Flag Committee's report could be tabled in the House of Commons, John Diefenbaker leapt to the attack. He probably hadn't seen the actual design, but he confidently charged it would be "indistinguishable from the flag of Peru." In fact, Peru's flag (*below*) shares neither the proportions nor the emblem of the winner.

The Tories, assuming the Liberals were still stuck on the prime minister's pennant, all voted for the single-leaf design, expecting a stalemate. To their astonishment, the ballots counted up at fourteen to zero. As Deachman would later write, "for a brief moment the choice of national flag was unanimous." The four English Tories were furious, but they had been outmanoeuvred. As previously agreed, the committee then voted to confirm its choice. This time the tally was ten to four. The lone Tory from Quebec, Théogène Ricard, had voted with the majority.

That evening, Monteith recorded in his diary, "the committee all repaired to Kingsmere where we really had an enjoyable evening at the Speaker's expense." Mackenzie King's cottage, high in the Gatineau Hills across the river from Ottawa, provided a safe place for the members to unwind. "After adequate dining and much wining," Matheson wrote, "we persuaded Margaret Konantz to remove one of the dark curtains from the window and costume herself as a medium. We then besought, with the aid of her crystal ball, the spirit of Mackenzie King and his revered mother."

The committee's final sessions settled the details of the report it would present to Parliament. But before this report could be tabled, any feelings of goodwill evaporated. First a leak of the final choice breached its carefully guarded confidentiality. Then Colonel Duguid, ever the stickler for heraldic minutiae, remarked that the flag they had chosen looked an awful lot like the flag of Peru. "People will say: 'Has Peru got a new colony?'" he suggested dismissively. John Diefenbaker immediately accepted Duguid's gift and went on television to denounce the single-leaf design as "indistinguishable from the flag of Peru." Then, on the morning of October 29, before Herman Batten could present the Flag Committee's recommendation to Parliament, the *Ottawa Citizen* published a front-page article by Grant Deachman, which purported to tell the behind-the-scenes story of how the flag was chosen.

At a different moment and in less loaded circumstances, Deachman's indiscretion might soon have been forgotten. But the former journalist had naively assumed his erstwhile colleagues of the press would hold the article until after the committee's

None of the MPs on the 1964 Flag Committee had been around Parliament long enough to recall Ephrem Côté's personal flag crusade of 1939, which he promoted by means of a self-published book, *Project of a Distinct National Flag for Canada,* and with "a souvenir button offered by the author to all members of the Ottawa Parliament." Like so many of Canada's flag missionaries before and after, Côté came up with an awkward compromise in an attempt to satisfy the French, the English and the others.

In the brief text outlining the case for his new flag, Côté recalled the enthusiasm of all Canadians during the recent royal visit of King George VI and Queen Elizabeth. "Nevertheless, one regret hovered over all Canada!" he wrote. "That of not having the consolation to see floating a real Canadian flag, [a] bilingual, official and distinct flag, amidst those banners that really merit to be unfurled in our country but that could not clearly distinguish us from other nations since they are truly not ours."

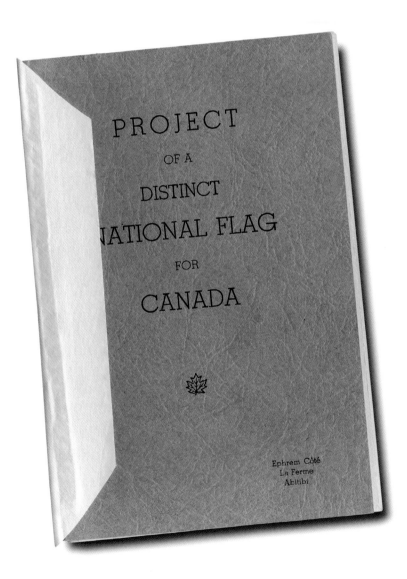

PROJECT OF A DISTINCT NATIONAL FLAG FOR CANADA

Ephrem Côté
La Ferme
Abitibi

Jacques Saint-Cyr's preliminary thirteen-point design and an eleven-point version (traced here from copies of the original) were included with a letter Patrick Reid addressed to John Matheson on November 9, 1964, but which was clearly intended for Privy Council Office eyes. "It is our opinion that one of the Saint-Cyr creations passes the distance test admirably ... It requires a slight strengthening of the two lower points of the leaf in order to be properly balanced in close-up ... All the other designs we have seen have, we feel, defects that may be difficult to retrieve. Any attempt to do so should be carried out by the originators."

> "The Committee, having been directed that there is to be no hauling down ceremony for the Red Ensign, strongly urges that reconsideration be given to the question of retiring the Canadian Red Ensign suitably, respectfully and with dignity."

Report of the interdepartmental committee charged with planning the inauguration of the new flag

report became public. No sooner had the House convened that day than the member from Vancouver Quadra stood up to apologize, but the damage had been done. Prudently, the Liberals decided to give everyone a month to cool off before the final Flag Debate would begin.

In the interim, the maple leaf flag needed to be finished. The final report described its design in principle but not in detail: "a red flag of the proportions two by length and one by width, containing at its centre a white square, the width of the flag, bearing a single red maple, or in heraldic terms, described as gules on a Canadian pale argent a maple leaf of the first." But which shade of red would the flag bear? And which maple leaf?

Once the Flag Committee had delivered its decision, the government raced to have a final design ready for what Pearson and Matheson still hoped would be fairly routine parliamentary passage. To help them accomplish this they turned to Patrick Reid, the commissioner of exhibitions for the federal government. He was the man responsible for every government display at international trade shows or world's

fairs. His department was already deep into its preparations for the fast-approaching Centennial Year. There's something poetically apt about Reid's role in the tale. He was, after all, a transplanted Irishman and by temperament an anti-bureaucrat, yet here he was being handed the job of refining – nay, perfecting – his adopted country's new flag. By his own account, he accepted the challenge with gusto.

Reid had on his staff some of the best designers in the business – and he would need them. Matheson, who acted as the informal liaison between the Privy Council Office and the Canadian Government Exhibition Commission, "was most concerned that we follow the model of the sugar maple leaf," Reid wrote in his memoirs. "It has 23 points and great vitality." But from Reid's perspective twenty-three points made for a design disaster: so busy that the leaf began to blur from more than a few feet away. Reid called in one of his top designers, Jacques Saint-Cyr, who readily agreed that twenty-three points were about ten too many. The irony was lost on neither of them that Saint-Cyr was a strong Quebec nationalist.

Saint-Cyr proceeded to rough out a much simpler design for a first meeting with Matheson, who liked Saint-Cyr's proposed thirteen-point leaf, a symmetrical shape which would make the two sides of the flag match perfectly. It was stylized but still evocative of the sugar maple. Saint-Cyr agreed to play with the thirteen-point design and produce several variations for their next meeting.

According to Reid, that meeting took place after business hours on Friday, November 6. In order to test how well the different designs worked at a distance, the three men moved to a long hallway, scurrying up and down its length to take turns observing the leaf as it would look waving atop a flagpole. None of Saint-Cyr's variants quite worked.

"Do you think maybe it's too busy at the base?" Reid asked after they'd been at this for some time. "What would happen, for example, if you took away two of the four points?"

The light bulb flicked on. Saint-Cyr immediately set about modifying his design, and within an hour he had a finished sketch that all three men approved.

This small souvenir Canadian ensign might have been waved at patriotic events anywhere in the Dominion during the nineteenth century. Note that the shield in the fly has an unusual embellishment, a wreath composed half of maple leaves, half of laurel.

It was already 10 p.m., and John Matheson headed home, exhausted from the long flag journey but elated that the new flag was so close to reality.

It is here that the story becomes murky, the recollections of the various participants often at odds with the established facts. Reid is adamant that three prototype versions of the eleven-point maple leaf flag were produced in the Commission's silkscreen shop that night and that one of these was "finished" by Joan O'Malley, the married daughter of Ken Donovan, one of Reid's employees. By around 2 a.m. on November 7, O'Malley had used the sewing machine she brought along to hem the flag and add a halyard, grommets and toggle so that it could be flown for prime ministerial approval that morning. Before dawn, Joan's father delivered the prototype to 24 Sussex Drive, the PM's residence. The following Monday, November 9, Pearson gave the eleven-pointed maple leaf his blessing. Cabinet endorsed the design soon after.

As for finding the right red, that proved surprisingly tricky. One of the more frivolous early objections to Pearson's proposed design had been the concern that its white

field would soon "look dirty." The advent of synthetic materials had made such objections obsolete, but as Reid discovered, a red that did not turn orange after a few days in the sun was hard to come by. In the end it required months of experiments and the assistance of the National Research Council to get it right.

That they had all got it right, history can attest. What's worth noting here is the complex collective process that led to such a remarkably simple and successful conclusion. Any number of people could and did claim to have "designed" the flag. Each of them made a contribution. But the truth is that the flag was designed over the couple of hundred years or more since a maple leaf first appeared as an emblem for something or someone Canadian, which originally meant Lower Canada but soon included Upper Canada. In the same sense that inventions cannot be invented until the world is ready for them – think of Leonardo da Vinci and his flying machine – the single maple leaf flag was out there, waiting to be discovered. The precise proportions and specific version of the leaf are ultimately beside the point. Through countless

FIRST AMONG MANY

The prototype flag preserved in the Queen's University Archives differs in one small but significant respect from the ultimate design. Note that the base of the maple leaf stem is cut at an angle, which meant that if exactly copied on the other side it wouldn't match. In the final version, Saint-Cyr cut the stem at a right angle, making the two sides identical.

THIRTY-FIVE YEARS after the adoption of the Maple Leaf, Glenn Wright, a senior archivist at Canada's national archives, set out to separate fact from fiction in the story of how Jacques Saint-Cyr's eleven-pointed maple leaf ended up on the flag. Wright's detective work highlighted many gaps and inconsistencies in the standard version of events.

For starters, on the night when Patrick Reid and others say the final flag design was born (November 6–7, 1964) John Matheson could only have been present if he was capable of time travel. Both his appointment diary and the next morning's edition of the *Kingston Whig-Standard* confirm he attended graduation ceremonies at a high school in Elgin, Ontario, about one hundred kilometres south of Ottawa. What's more, in the letter Reid wrote to Matheson, dated November 9, 1964, he refers to "one of the Saint-Cyr creations... presented in flag form to the Prime Minister last Friday," which was November 6, not 7.

Even more telling are Joan O'Malley's recollections of the night her sewing skills were called upon. She says she finished not one flag design but two copies each of three designs, designs suspiciously similar to ones being considered by the Flag Committee in early October. Furthermore the cloth on which these six flags were printed was thick and very difficult for her machine to sew, while the sole surviving Saint-Cyr prototype is printed on light-weight cheesecloth.

What really happened? Perhaps two distinct episodes have been conflated into a single, more dramatic tale. In the two-part scenario, Joan O'Malley's sewing skills are called upon in early October when it's clear there isn't enough Flag Committee support for Pearson's Pennant. John Matheson asks Patrick Reid to produce flag versions of three of the more plausible alternatives. These are silkscreened onto thick cloth and hemmed by O'Malley. Matheson shows them to the prime minister, who indicates he is open to something other than his personal choice.

A few weeks later, in early November, the Prime Minister's Office (PMO) asks Reid to work on the single-leaf flag's final design. Over one long night – almost certainly not November 6–7 Jacques Saint-Cyr comes up with the elegant eleven-point variation. A silkscreened example is delivered to the PMO on Friday, November 6.

If so, then two of the three original silkscreened prototypes aren't missing at all. They were never made. The flag that was sent to Pearson for approval on November 6 is the same flag Matheson later gave to Queen's, and today the university archives house an artifact even more precious than anyone realized.

"Mr. Speaker, I plead with all the members of this House to put an end to this debate. Let us behave like reasonable and mature adults and bring this question once and for all to a decision. I am sure that is what our constituents expect of us."

MARGARET KONANTZ, MP, during the final hours of the Flag Debate, December 14, 1964

conscious and unconscious choices, Canadians had designed their own flag. And now it was about to become official.

ON THE MORNING of November 30, following speeches in honour of Winston Churchill's ninetieth birthday, the final phase of the Flag Debate got off to a rocky start when the leader of the opposition rose on a point of privilege. John Diefenbaker's words seemed innocent enough. During the important debate about to commence, would the prime minister, he wondered, "permit orders of the day to be called to provide an opportunity for the asking and answering of questions, and that thereafter we revert to motions?" Behind the parliamentary language, however, the Chief was actually firing a warning shot across the Liberal bow: *You may think the final flag debate is going to be smooth sailing, but I plan to fight you to the finish.* According to the rules, rules Diefenbaker knew by heart, no Question Period was permitted while a motion was under debate. Diefenbaker thus served notice that it would be quite a few days before any questions were going to be asked, because he intended to stretch the debate to its limit and the

government to the breaking point.

After considering the point of privilege raised by the leader of the opposition, the Speaker ruled against it, forcing the Tory plans for prolonging the debate out into the open. Diefenbaker now asked the Speaker to rule that before the House could consider the Flag Committee report, it needed to debate the original motion of June 15 calling for the Pearson Pennant, which was still on the order paper and had never come to a vote. The Speaker reserved his decision on this point until the following day, when he ruled in Diefenbaker's favour. With the government opposing its original motion, it easily went down to defeat. Now the Tory filibuster was on: the seemingly interminable Flag Debate of the summer looked set to start all over again.

Diefenbaker was daring Pearson to invoke closure – the only way to arbitrarily close off debate and force a vote. In so doing he was deliberately evoking memories of the infamous Pipeline Debate of 1956, when the St. Laurent government's attempt to ram through an important piece of legislation left the Liberals looking both out of touch and dictatorial. Diefenbaker's stellar performance during the debate helped him win the party leadership at the Tory convention later that year, and he'd used the pipeline issue at every campaign stop during the election that followed. In the fall of 1964, the Tory leader knew he did not have the votes to defeat the government on the flag issue, since both the NDP and the Créditistes supported the new flag. He believed, however, that he could force the government to withdraw the motion rather than drop the guillotine of closure.

The fourteen days that followed were among the ugliest in House of Commons history. The Tory members of the Flag Committee, who might have sat quietly while their leader fulminated against the committee's choice, were too humiliated and angered by what they regarded as Liberal betrayal to sit on the sidelines. They spoke repeatedly and heatedly, especially Waldo Monteith, who had taken the whole thing quite personally. As the filibuster dragged on, Speaker Macnaughton proved incapable of enforcing the relevancy rule that required members' speeches to bear at least some glancing connection to the motion under discussion. It became a question of

The maple leaf on the front cover was red and so were quite a few faces at *Weekend Magazine* when the popular Saturday supplement, which appeared in newspapers across Canada on January 23, 1965, flew the wrong flag. This was the earlier thirteen-point version, not the final eleven-point design. On Monday, January 25, the *Weekend* switchboard "exploded with calls asking why our flag on the cover had 13 points." Sacks of mail soon followed. Which all went to prove "that the pundits who claimed Canadians were bored with the flag shenanigans are dead wrong. Canadians are very much aware they have a new flag, and take a passionate interest in it."

The royal proclamation of the new Canadian flag is dated January 28, 1965, "in the thirteenth Year of Our Reign" and signed by Lester B. Pearson, prime minister of Canada, "By Her Majesty's Command." The original document resides at the National Archives in Ottawa, where it is stored in a specially constructed case that filters out ultraviolet light and monitors the minutest change in its microenvironment.

who would give in first, the government or the opposition.

But Diefenbaker had counted too much on the loyalty and discipline of his caucus, a good number of whom were itching for his ouster. In the end it was his Quebec lieutenant, Léon Balcer, who broke the stalemate. On Wednesday, December 9, Balcer rose on a point of personal privilege. After lamenting the long paralysis of the House because of the flag issue and reminding his fellow MPs that the length of the debate had afforded ample opportunity for every opinion to be heard, he invited the government to invoke closure. "I believe that it is my duty to ... invite the Prime Minister, or one of his Ministers, to give notice that he will make use of Standing Order 33 to have this question settled without further delay by applying the rule of closure."

In effect, Balcer was telling the House and the Tory opposition that Diefenbaker had lost the confidence of his caucus and that his leadership was in doubt. In those few words, Balcer transformed the Flag Debate from a parliamentary wrangle into the act of nation-building it might always

have been. Now the only question was how soon the government would force the vote and how large the majority in favour of the new flag would be.

The final division of the House of Commons on the flag question occurred at 2:15 a.m. on December 15, 1964, almost exactly six months after Pearson had delivered his fine debate-opening speech. The prime minister made the issue a free vote, meaning all members could vote as their consciences dictated, even if their consciences were contrary to their party's position. But he pleaded unsuccessfully for the vote to be unrecorded: Diefenbaker was determined to count the number of his friends and enemies. Nonetheless many Conservatives – including all the French-speaking ones, among them Léon Balcer and Théogène Ricard – voted with the government, as did the majority of Socreds and New Democrats. The motion passed, 163 to 78. (Only one Liberal, Ralph Cowan, voted against.)

As soon as the tally was announced, a rising Liberal star from Quebec, Yvon Dupuis, stood up and led members on both sides of the aisle in lusty versions of "O Canada,"

The ceremonies for the new flag held in Ottawa on February 15, 1965, commenced shortly after 11 a.m. beneath the ornate, neo-Gothic vault of the Hall of Honour with speeches by Governor General Georges Vanier (*centre*), Prime Minister Lester Pearson (left of Vanier) and the Speakers of the Senate and the House of Commons. John Diefenbaker (standing at right between his wife, Olive, and Pauline Vanier) had been invited to say a few words but declined. (To the left of Pearson stand his wife, Maryon, and Maurice Bourget, Speaker of the Senate.)

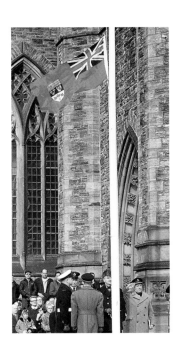

The Canadian Red Ensign flies one last time on Parliament Hill before being slowly lowered and carried away. The large crowd that had been waiting on the snow-crusted lawns for more than an hour was about to see some history being made.

which would not become Canada's official national anthem until 1980. Then most of those present sang "God Save the Queen." A few Tories sat shell-shocked in their seats, like hockey players who had just lost the deciding game of a Stanley Cup final. John Matheson was too choked up to sing, but he stood with happy tears streaming down his face.

After the House adjourned, Liberal campaign guru Keith Davey, who'd been observing the proceedings from the gallery, bumped into Pearson as he was returning to his office. Davey had been carried away by the import of the evening's events. Pearson was the acme of cool.

"Keith, imagine. John Matheson down there blubbering," the prime minister commented. Pearson seemed to be putting the flag flap behind him already. But Davey was unable to speak.

TWO MONTHS LATER to the day, on the morning of February 15, 1965, a surprisingly large crowd – given that it was a weekday in winter – gathered on Parliament Hill in damp, bitter cold and fitful sunshine to witness the first official raising of Canada's new maple leaf flag. Those who'd received invitations to hear the speeches in the Hall of Honour listened first to Governor General Georges Vanier, who'd fought in the First World War and commanded Quebec's fabled Van Doo (the Royal 22nd Regiment). Then Lester Pearson gave a brief but stirring speech, displaying an emotion he rarely revealed in public. He concluded, "Under this Flag may our youth find new inspiration for loyalty to Canada; for patriotism based not on any mean or narrow nationalism, but on the deep and equal pride that all Canadians will feel for every part of this good land. God bless our Flag! And God bless Canada!"

Accompanied by an honour guard resplendent in bearskin hats and slate-grey greatcoats, the dignitaries then trooped out of the Centre Block to stand on the special dais set up in front of the Peace Tower with a temporary flagpole, from which the Red Ensign limply hung.

People had been waiting patiently on the crusty old snow that covered the lawn in front of the Parliament Buildings. Some had brought maple leaf flags to wave; many carried home-movie cameras. At least one

As if some celestial puppeteer were pulling the strings, when the new flag reached the top of the flagpole, a breeze rippled it prettily. "And the feelings that a flag is a flag is a flag," wrote journalist George Bain, "which had attacked both partisans of change and defenders of the old before the long debate was finished, were dispelled, because it looked bold and clean, and distinctively our own."

Almost from the first moment the new flag flew, it looked right. As Jacques Saint-Cyr and Patrick Reid had hoped, Canada's "Maple Leaf" read well at a distance and up close. There was little question: this flag was a keeper.

held a Red Ensign draped in black. The politicians and the ordinary citizens watched quietly as the old flag, the Canadian Red Ensign, which had flown from federal buildings as a temporary measure since 1945, was officially lowered for the last time and carefully folded by members of the Canadian Armed Forces, while chaplains intoned prayers in French and English.

Then the old flag departed to the safekeeping of the registrar general and the new flag was brought forward by three non-commissioned officers, one from each of the three armed services, who unfolded it and waited while more prayers were said. They fastened the red-white-red rectangle to the lanyard on the bare white flagpole. Slowly they raised it up the mast to the strains of "O Canada." Just as it reached the top, "emotions that had been pent up for more than an hour erupted into a mighty cheer," in the words of one observer. The wind was barely enough to make it stir during the twenty-one-gun salute, but as the salute ended a breeze sprang up and caught the Maple Leaf flag that had been raised simultaneously from the East Block, stretching it out into a red-and-white ex-

clamation point in the now-clearing sky. Then the wind caught another flag, and another and another until the Maple Leaf was flying from every tower on Parliament Hill – except the Peace Tower, from which the governor general's dark blue standard waved – and the sun obligingly lit them all.

Throughout the ceremony the leaders of Canada's federal political parties stood near one another on the platform. Stone-faced and still, John Diefenbaker did not lift his eyes as the smart red-white-red banner snapped in the freshening breeze. A few of those near him noted that his eyes brimmed with tears.

Those who gazed upward remembered the moment always. To them the new flag looked … right. It looked like a country coming into its own.

"The struggle for a Canadian flag presents in conflict two prime ministers and Canadian statesmen, John George Diefenbaker, steadfast, immovable, courageous, abounding in loyalty and zeal, and Lester Bowles Pearson, a gentle and heroic patriot, full of charity and kindness ... The real paradox of this tale is that it was John Diefenbaker, of whose love for Canada there is no question, who fought against Canada's flag. It was Lester Pearson, who philosophically would have pulled down all flags everywhere, who showed his raw love of his country by producing the symbol of Canada's yearning to survive."

JOHN ROSS MATHESON, in his introduction to *Canada's Flag: A Search for a Country*, 1986

CHAPTER FOUR

Maple leaf rising

THE DAY the Canadian Red Ensign was lowered for the last time and the first red-and-white Maple Leaf went up the special flagstaff erected in front of the Peace Tower on Parliament Hill, similar ceremonies took place at federal buildings across the country, on Canadian ships at sea and at Canadian embassies and consulates around the world. The ceremonies were held at noon in each time zone, making for a slow-motion sequence of flag raisings that circumnavigated the globe. The first Maple Leaf of the day was raised somewhere west of the international date line. The flag raisings then proceeded westward with the noonday sun, time zone by time zone, to Auckland and Canberra, Tokyo and Manila, Beijing and Phnom Penh, Delhi and Islamabad, before stepping across central Asia to the capitals of continental Europe, and then to London. From the British Isles, the flag hopped from Canadian merchant vessel to navy ship and made its first appearance at Reykjavik, Iceland, before it once again reached continental terra firma.

In Canada, the first flag raising took place in Charlottetown, Prince Edward Island, which held its ceremony at 10 a.m. and so got a head start on St. John's, New-foundland, which could ordinarily count on being half an hour ahead of everybody else in the country. But given Newfound-land premier Joey Smallwood's opposition to the new flag, he was in no hurry. At noon the premier and a few members of the legislature emerged from the Confed-eration Building to sullenly observe two Canadian flags ascending two temporary flagpoles. The usually loquacious politician retreated inside without saying a word. In Halifax, a huge Maple Leaf was raised up what was claimed to be the tallest flagpole in the Commonwealth, located on the Grand Parade in front of City Hall, while a band played "The Maple Leaf Forever."

From the Atlantic coast the official flag raisings proceeded toward the Pacific. At Queen's Park in Toronto a crowd of two thousand listened but did not sing as "God Save the Queen" accompanied the new flag up the mast. But after the twenty-one-gun salute they joined in the singing of "O Can-ada" and cheered. In Edmonton, the weath-er was so cold that the ceremony had to be held inside. Outside the British Columbia legislature in Victoria, only four people, none of them elected members, braved the

A happy crowd on Parlia-ment Hill on April 17, 1982 (*opposite*), celebrates the ceremonial signing of the Constitution Act by Queen Elizabeth II and Prime Minister Pierre Elliott Trudeau, which finally brought the Can-adian constitution home. The flag they waved in celebration was not yet twenty years old.

February 15, 1965, was an emotional day for Canadians around the world as the familiar Red Ensign was lowered for the last time and the new Maple Leaf was raised up hundreds of official flagpoles and many unofficial ones on land and at sea. *Left to right*: the Red Ensign comes down at the Canadian embassy in Hong Kong; a simultaneous lowering and raising aboard HMCS *Fraser*; the new flag nears the top of the flagpole during the grandiose official ceremony at Queen's Park in Toronto.

Surrounded by young fans of the new flag in St. Jean Baptiste, Manitoba, on October 7, 1965, Prime Minister Lester Pearson looks to have shed a few of his sixty-eight years. Of all his accomplishments while in office, which included the Canada Pension Plan, the Royal Commission on Bilingualism and Biculturalism, the Canada Health Act and the integration of the armed forces, the flag can be seen as his crowning legacy. His biographer John English quotes Pearson's wife, Maryon, as saying, "The flag was the achievement he prized most."

   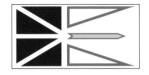

deliberately inconvenient dawn hour of the new flag's first raising. A few days earlier, Premier W.A.C. Bennett's cabinet had passed an order-in-council directing that "the Canadian Red Ensign be appropriately displayed on all suitable occasions in the Province of British Columbia in addition to the National Flag of Canada."

British Columbia and Prince Edward Island were not alone in breaking with the noon protocol. The Canadian high commissioner to Jamaica chose to hold his ceremony at a more temperate 5 p.m., followed by a cocktail reception for all the island's Canadian residents. As the Red Ensign came down for the last time, they sang "Auld Lang Syne." According to one press report, there were approximately sixteen hundred official raisings of the new flag around the world that day. No one tried to count the unofficial ones, many of them by necessity involving unofficial flags. (The demand had far outstripped the supply, forcing many schools and businesses to keep flying the Red Ensign or fly nothing.) In Stayner, a small town just south of Collingwood, Ontario, a local high school student solved the shortage by gluing red

cutouts of the leaf and bars to a white bed-sheet. In some places flags with a thirteen-pointed leaf were raised in error: these flags had been made in Japan by manufacturers who had jumped the gun before the eleven-point design was final.

It was not only at the country's two most British extremes, Victoria and St. John's, that the new flag faced inclement weather. Paul Delaney, a politically engaged history major at Trent University in Peterborough, Ontario, recalls observing an anti-flag-raising event that evening. The protest flag bore a single blue fleur-de-lys against a white field flanked by two blue bars, reflecting, he says, "the widespread feeling that Pearson's Liberals were appeasing Quebec at the expense of Canada's heritage."

Ultimately, four provinces managed to hang on to some version of the old flag. In Manitoba and Ontario, Tory premiers Duff Roblin and John Robarts soon unveiled as their provincial flags Red Ensigns with the provincial arms in the fly. The province of Newfoundland, which only eighteen years before had been a British colony, retained the Union Jack as its flag, allowing Joey to keep his promise. British Columbia

"From British sea to British sea" seems like the collective message of these four provincial flags (*left to right*): British Columbia, Manitoba, Ontario and Newfoundland. British Columbia's was adopted in 1960. Manitoba and Ontario acquired theirs immediately after the Canadian Red Ensign was displaced by the Maple Leaf. Newfoundland retained the British Union Jack until 1980, when it adopted this beautifully stylized version of the jack designed by artist Christopher Pratt. All four flags are still flying, firm reminders of the British past that underlies the English-Canadian present.

"There is nothing in this of turning backs on a hated past, nothing suggesting that old ties were irksome. The point is simply that the country is growing up, coming to see itself as an entity, taking the interest in itself that any organism, to be healthy, must."

Historian ARTHUR LOWER, commenting on the rapid acceptance of the Maple Leaf

New flag supply couldn't keep up with new flag demand once the Maple Leaf became official. A federal government employee (*opposite*) packs some of the thousands of flags that would fly from government buildings throughout Canada.

already had a flag based on its coat of arms, combining a stretched-out Union Jack with a sun setting over the Pacific. As civil disobedience goes, these acts of protest were not much, but the message they sent was similar to the one expressed in many editorial and opinion pieces and in quite a few private conversations on the day after the new flag was first raised: *You've trampled on our traditions.*

In Quebec, the first flags flew in more ominous breezes. When the Maple Leaf was hoisted outside the legislature, separatist protesters started to boo. Some shouted, "Down with the Maple Leaf, long live the Fleur-de-lys!" At the official ceremony inside, Premier Jean Lesage sounded an optimistic note, saying, "Let this flag be the rallying symbol of all Canadians, from one ocean to the other." The next day in Montreal, however, demonstrators in front of a French-language radio station that had raised the new flag (and lowered the Quebec flag) burned a Maple Leaf in protest. And opposition leader Daniel Johnson of the Union Nationale threw salt into old wounds by declaring, "I hope that one day, over the parliament of a resolutely bi-national

Canada, the symbols of the two language and cultural communities which work together for the greatness and prosperity of our beautiful country will fly side by side."

Wherever the British connection was strongest – including the regions settled and shaped by the United Empire Loyalists – as many or more Canadian Red Ensigns flew after February 15 as before. In these areas it was hard to find a maple leaf flag beyond those that fluttered from federal courthouses and post offices, from prisons and unemployment offices. Many chapters of the Royal Canadian Legion kept the Red Ensign flying. (Within a year, however, the Legion had officially endorsed the Maple Leaf.)

Protest came also from Sir Anthony Wagner, England's Garter King of Arms, head of all British heralds. No sooner was the Maple Leaf flag proclaimed than Sir Anthony wrote an acid letter to Gordon Robertson, Canada's clerk of the Privy Council, to complain that he had not been consulted before the flag became official. Furthermore, he took issue with the term "Canadian pale," as the Flag Committee had described the middle panel, remarking

IN THE MID-1960s the Grandstand Show at the annual Canadian National Exhibition (CNE) was just about the biggest show in town. Every evening during the two-week run of Toronto's overgrown fall fair, thousands of people packed the football stadium on the CNE grounds for a variety extravaganza headlined by big-name stars. In August – September 1965 those stars were as big as they come: Victor Borge and Bob Hope.

But the heart of the show was the homegrown talent: the Canadiana Symphony Orchestra led by the irrepressible Howard Cable (still actively composing and conducting when this book went to press in 2008) and a female chorus of dancers called the Canadettes. The evening's grand finale was a huge production number choreographed by Alan and Blanche Lund performed to a song written by Stan Daniels especially for the occasion. Appropriately, given that 1965 was

the year Canada finally adopted a flag, the song was "You've Got a Flag – Wave It!" The melody was only pleasant and the lyrics merely pedestrian, but the song caught the mood of the moment – enough so that Columbia Records released a 45 rpm recording. (The record's flip side features Debbie Lorrie Kaye backed by the Howard Cable Orchestra and Chorus in another Stan Daniel's tune: "I Wanna Hear That New Sound.") Those were the days!

The new flag meant boom times for Canada's flag manufacturers. Here a worker checks for flaws in the silkscreening as new Maple Leafs roll off a line at Dominion Flag in the east end of Toronto.

that it was "a phrase not previously known to me as a term of heraldry."

The term "Canadian pale" was the brainchild of Conrad Swan, Rouge Dragon of the College of Arms and thus Sir Anthony's subordinate. Swan, born in Canada, had every right to advise Beddoe and Matheson, and no doubt he took issue with his superior's assertion that "the name of Canada has become associated with a heraldic joke"; but if he did, he did so privately. Sir Anthony also asked Robertson to "remit the sum of one hundred guineas ... to cover both work done in the past and registration now proposed." Canada's most eminent civil servant seems to have briefly considered ignoring this request, but he paid the fee rather than give Sir Anthony more cause for complaint. Lionel Chevrier, then Canada's high commissioner in London, described the whole thing as a "tempest in a teapot." So it was. Yet for all its silliness it demonstrates how badly the Maple Leaf flag was needed as an emblem of genuine independence.

Far more Canadians welcomed the new emblem than resisted it. Demand for it was instant and massive. It would be several months before new flag supply caught up with new flag demand. Especially in the country's ethnically diverse cities, the Maple Leaf began to flap from front-yard flagpoles and to hang from apartment balconies. On July 1, 1965, the first Dominion Day celebration where people could wave a Maple Leaf nationwide, many thousands of Canadians did exactly that. The new flag inspired at least one patriotic song, "The Flag of Canada," with words and music by Freddy Grant. Neither the words nor the music gave Alexander Muir much competition, but they were nonetheless heartfelt.

When I gaze on the flag of our nation,
There's a wonderful vision I see,
Of a future grand in a growing land.
With each creed and race marching hand
    in hand,
Under one command, as our founders
    planned,
That's what Canada's flag means to me.

In remarkably short order the new flag seems to have become a non-issue for most Canadians. In an end-of-year interview with the prime minister, not a question was asked about the flag and not a comment was

The first registered Canadian trademark to employ Canada's emerging national emblem was the Maple Leaf Brand trademark of the Victoria Canning Company of British Columbia, registered in 1895. But before 1895 there were probably many hundreds of unregistered commercial insignia that marked their wares with the sign of the maple leaf.

These three cloth patches date from the 1950s *(left)* through to the present day *(right)*. They were and are worn on coats and jackets as signs of affiliation or souvenirs of travel.

offered. Blair Fraser, the long-time editor of *Maclean's*, aptly summed up the general view in his book *The Search for Identity: Canada, 1945–1967*: "The whole fuss seemed to have been forgotten within weeks. An issue which had terrified Canadian governments for forty years, and been a burr under Canada's saddle for a century, had at last been disposed of forever." Well, perhaps not completely disposed of.

John Diefenbaker persevered as Tory leader, nursing a sense of betrayal on behalf of those who honoured the British connection. In a television address he delivered on CBC's *The Nation's Business* two days after the flag ceremony, he was unrepentant: "In the last few days events took place not only on Parliament Hill but across Canada. We have got a new flag. As leader of Her Majesty's Loyal Opposition, and as an officer of Parliament, I was present at the raising of that flag. It was my duty to be there because I believe in Parliament. I confess, too, that I had a heavy heart. I did not know until I read it – I was not aware that tears fell from my eyes until I saw the picture. But I cannot change my convictions."

Even more revealing than the words he

broadcast are some of the words he edited out of the speech before delivery: "It was for me, and I am sure for many Canadians, a sad occasion. It was particularly sad for those of us who had fought long and hard for the retention of the symbols of our history and culture in the flag." A second deletion hinted that in Dief's mind, at least, the fight was not over: "I do not wish to renew that controversy now or to cast any aspersions on the new flag, which is, after all that has been said and done, the flag of Canada as of this moment."

As of this moment. As if it might be possible to turn back the clock when it seemed to be ticking ever faster toward the day of Diefenbaker's departure. Following the Tory leader's performance in the December Flag Debate and the deep divisions in his caucus it had exposed, most observers agreed that Dief's days were numbered. Léon Balcer, who had broken with his leader on the flag issue, would soon leave the Tory caucus, then quit politics altogether. Most pundits dismissed Diefenbaker as yesterday's man. So did the governing Liberals who, in early October 1965, called a snap election for November 8.

The Mountie Quilt (left) was made by Beth Craig of Delta, Ontario, in 1975 to honour Canada's famous scarlet-uniformed police. The caption that accompanies this quilt at the Canadian Museum of Civilization reads in part, "Craig was inspired to the task because she felt that children should be taught that Mounties have exceptional qualities – knowledge and love of nature, bravery and fairness. Part cowboy, part Boy Scout and part soldier, the Mountie is the symbolic embodiment of the highest Canadian values." *Beaver Eating a Maple Leaf (above)* is considerably more ambiguous, especially given its intended use as a weather vane, which shifts direction with the wind.

Canadians have an interesting relationship with heroes. They invented one of the most famous comic book superheroes (Superman) yet they tend to tear down real-life heroes whenever they get too full of themselves. In the early 1940s, homegrown comic book heroes flourished, including Nelvana of the Northern Lights and Johnny Canuck. After American competition closed down most Canadian comic book publishing in 1947, these mythic figures disappeared until the 1970s, when they often reappeared in satiric guises, poking fun at the whole genre. One of the first of this new breed was Winnipeg artist Ron Leishman's Captain Canuck, the first superhero to wrap himself in the new flag.

A more recent Canadian-born superhero is Northguard, who first appeared in 1984 (*right*). The plot of this novel-length comic book brings Northguard (a young comic book fan named Phillip Wise) into a deadly struggle with ManDes, a conflation of "Manifest Destiny" who clearly stands for the worst of the United States of America.

Pearson and his advisers hoped to capitalize on Tory disarray and on what they believed was a desire for parliamentary stability to achieve the majority that had eluded them in 1963. One might have expected the Liberal campaign to have draped itself in the flag, one of the few solid achievements of Pearson's short first term in office, but it would seem the Liberal strategists completely ignored it. The wounds were still too raw.

At the start of the campaign, the Liberals led in the polls by 20 percentage points, with the support of 48 percent of the electorate to the Tories' 28 percent (if the undecided were distributed in the same proportion as the decided). As far as Mike Pearson was concerned, the election was in the bag, even though a remarkable 36 percent of voters had not yet made up their minds. John Diefenbaker went to work persuading them.

As in 1963, and as if to thumb his nose at modernity, the Chief campaigned by train for most of his tour, moving from event to event with a ferocious energy that belied his seventy years. And as they had in 1963, when Diefenbaker had denied Pearson his majority, the crowds grew larger and more enthusiastic as he went. The Tory leader was in his element on the stump, playing up Liberal arrogance and ridiculing the needlessness of the election call. By the time his tour reached his traditional stomping ground in the Prairies, he clearly had the momentum. He knew how to play those western crowds like a concertmaster with a Stradivarius. And only in his speeches out west did his campaign tune occasionally include a few bars about the flag.

On the night Diefenbaker spoke in Penticton, British Columbia, he paid homage to the service rendered by local MP David Pugh and the other Tories on the Flag Committee, using it as a segue into one of his favourite podium routines out west: "Within two weeks after the new flag was declared officially for Canada, the Ottawa Liberal Association [and] the University Association of Canada came out for the abolition of the Queen." Then he asked his audience to pull out their new social insurance cards, which had formerly borne the coat of arms of Canada with its Union Jack and royal crown. "Today you have a new card on which the crown has been removed and

By 1979, the year of John Diefenbaker's last campaign, the flag furore of the 1960s seemed like ancient history. Even Dief's personal campaign poster used a maple leaf to send its patriotic message.

the coat of arms," he would say, implying there was a Liberal plot to get rid of the monarchy and turn the country into a republic. "Where will they go next? They didn't bring the flag question in front of the people in the last election. Where will they go?"

The 1965 campaign would be John Diefenbaker's last as leader and he made the most of it. By the time the results were in on the evening of November 8, the Tories had gained an astonishing 13 percentage points over where they had stood the day the vote was called, one of the greatest recorded gains over the course of a campaign since the birth of election polling. Dief had not only prevented Pearson from reaching the majority he coveted, he had managed to lead his party to a gain of two seats over its 1963 total.

To explain such a shift in voter support, one must surely look for something deeper than Diefenbaker's legendary campaign legerdemain. Is it only coincidence that this remarkable comeback took place within months of the official arrival of the Maple Leaf? If you drew a demographic map of how the country voted in 1965, you would notice

that the parts of the country painted Tory blue lay overwhelmingly outside the great urban areas and were for the most part strikingly British in profile. By contrast, the big cities and the French-speaking regions of the country were painted more or less entirely Liberal, new-flag red.

Seen in this light, Dief's amazing comeback looks at least in part like a protest vote by the Canada that had fought without question for the Empire in the Boer War and had unhesitatingly joined the Imperial brigades on the Western Front in 1914. Conversely, it highlighted the difficult birth pangs of the new, late-twentieth-century Canada that was struggling into being.

The 1965 election marked a watershed in Canadian politics, the last fought by Liberal and Tory leaders born in the nineteenth century, both of whom had served in the First World War. Neither of them fully understood the emerging country each fought to lead. How could they? The country did not understand itself. But now both Pearson and Diefenbaker were fading from the scene. Within three years of their final standoff, new men would replace them, men born in the twentieth century

Pierre Elliott Trudeau acknowledges the cheers of his supporters during the Liberal Party leadership convention held in Ottawa in April 1968. Five years earlier, before his election to Parliament as one of the "three wise men" recruited from Quebec by Lester Pearson, he'd been a political unknown. But in the aftermath of Expo 67, the young(ish), fluently bilingual bachelor seemed to personify Canada's newly self-confident spirit. As the convention proved, he was far more popular in the country than in the party. He won narrowly against a powerful field of Pearson cabinet ministers on the fourth ballot.

who had come of age between the two world wars. And one of them, in 1965 a freshman MP from Montreal, would emerge as the leader who perfectly caught the spirit of the times.

In his first election campaign as leader of the Liberal Party, the Trudeaumania election of 1968, Pierre Elliott Trudeau seemed to answer the yearning of an increasingly urban, economically robust and youth-oriented country to embrace the present. He timed his arrival perfectly, winning a leadership convention held only a few months after the close of the year of Centennial celebrations crowned by the most successful world exposition ever. During Expo 67 in Montreal, Canadians suddenly discovered they were good at something and were actually interesting – "groovy" – to the rest of the world. And a swinging bachelor seemed like the natural selection at this stage of the country's evolution. Would Pierre Trudeau have been the Liberal choice before Expo? Probably not. And would Expo, which very nearly didn't happen, have miraculously come together in a country that hadn't recently adopted its own flag? It's hard to imagine.

Even Expo 67's official title, Man and His World, suggested the psychic shift that accompanied Canada's Centennial feel-good session. The world's fair, built on two artificial islands in the St. Lawrence River in Montreal, was an instant hit with visitors and introduced novel architectural ideas that are with us still. One of the most eye-catching structures on the Île Sainte-Hélène site (*left*) was the inverted pyra-mid called Katimavik, which means "meet-ing place" in the Inuit language. Two Centen-nial medallions (*above*) corroborate the theory that in a sense the new flag made Expo possible. On one (*left*), Pearson's great accomplishment is celebrated; on the other (*right*), the simplifed leaf motif designed as the Centennial logo is un-equivocally linked with the Maple Leaf flag.

> "Expo 67 was the greatest birthday party in history, but for those willing to learn it was also an education. For one beautiful, unforgettable summer, Expo took us into the future that can be ours."
>
> ROBERT FULFORD, journalist and critic

An unidentified Canadian soldier stands guard in front of a building on Canadian Forces Base Valcartier, just outside Quebec City, on October 12, 1970 (*opposite*). During the dark days of the October Crisis, Canadians – especially those dwelling in Ottawa, Montreal and Quebec City – lived under a state of siege that made their democratic institutions seem perilously fragile.

Canada's hundredth-birthday emblem, a cleverly simplified maple leaf built out of eleven identical equilateral triangles, was endlessly reproduced in countless Centennial projects (and in the cement of new city sidewalks) in towns and villages and hamlets across the land. It made a perfect logo that was a lot easier for a school kid to draw than the maple leaf on the flag. Now try to imagine what our Centennial symbol would have looked like if we had adopted the Red Ensign as our official banner. Two buck-toothed beavers playing hockey in a birchbark canoe?

In the two years between the birth of the Maple Leaf and the start of Canada's hundredth-birthday bash, many observers noted that Canadians had started to think differently about their country. It has been said that a country is an act of the imagination. Before the Maple Leaf, the country of Expo 67 and of glamorous, Gallic Pierre Trudeau would have been much more difficult to conjure. After the Maple Leaf, anything seemed possible, and for at least those twelve months of 1967 – and above all that golden Expo spring and summer – Canadians imagined the world.

As deep as the crises in Confederation have been since Lester Pearson gave us our flag, the single maple leaf's signal success is that it has always stood for something greater than the sum of our two founding nations. Trudeau himself might have admitted as much, even if, before he became an instant Liberal so that he could run for Parliament, he had ridiculed Pearson's flag quest as irrelevant, saying, "Quebec doesn't give a tinker's damn about the new flag, it's a matter of complete indifference." But the stubborn beliefs he brought to government and never relinquished were remarkably in sync with the unitary symbolism of the single maple leaf flag: no to narrow, ethnically defined nationalism; yes to a pluralistic, multivalent society. To accomplish his anti-nationalist vision of nationhood, Trudeau believed he had to make Canada's French fact a necessary reality for all Canadians, while giving his fellow Québécois a sense of belonging to the whole country.

In the attempt to impose official bilingualism, he satisfied few and alienated many. In his overreaction to the October Crisis of 1970, he radicalized a whole generation of Québécois. But in the long run the

You can tell that Calgarian Jeff Liberty made it onto Canada's 2000 swim team by the two tattoos on his chest. The maple leaf meant he'd qualified for the national team; the Olympic rings were added when he went to Sydney, Australia. No one seems to be sure which Canadian swimmer started the team's ritual of patriotic body embellishment, but it seems all the swimmers joined in. As for Liberty, a three-metre diver, he won no medals at the Sydney Olympics but earned a higher honour later when he rescued a pregnant woman from her car after it plunged into the icy Bow River.

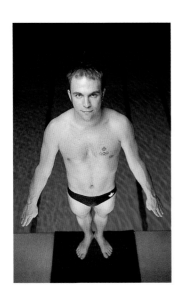

vision that underlay these measures would prevail. Trudeau's idea of "one Canada" would change us in profound and permanent ways.

After Expo and with Trudeau so stylishly in power, most Canadians soon forgot there had ever been a fight over the flag. Most – but not all. Ten years after Expo, heraldic expert Conrad Swan could write in his book *Canada: Symbols of Sovereignty*, "Without a doubt, the one aspect of heraldry in Canada which seems guaranteed to raise heat under collars in the shortest possible time is the National Flag, and it appears to be too soon, even yet, to be able to discuss the flag dispassionately in most general circles throughout the country." Swan cannot have spent much time mingling with the thousands of Canadian students who backpacked through Europe in the late 1960s and early 1970s. It would have been hard to find a single rucksack without a maple leaf flag sewn on it in a declaration of nationality. The flag also made a difference for Canada's distinguished contingent of foreign correspondents. Knowlton Nash, who dodged bullets during the American intervention in the Dominican Republic in 1965, recalls that after he and his colleagues started wearing the new flag, "you were a lot less likely to get shot at."

Another sign that the Maple Leaf was here to stay was the way it became part of our culture, highbrow and lowbrow. Artist and filmmaker Joyce Wieland wrapped herself in a Canadian flag in front of the Canadian consulate in New York as an aesthetic protest against the war in Vietnam, and she played patriotic variations on its theme in her 1967 painting *Confedspread* and in her 1970 – 71 series, *Flag Arrangement*. In the late 1970s, Charles Pachter, who has made a specialty of ringing visual changes on Canadian icons ranging from moose to Mounties, began his eye-catching series *The Painted Flags*, a series he is still adding to. Comedians Johnny Wayne and Frank Shuster posed with a globe over which they'd raised a satiric Canadian flag of conquest: Pax Canadiana? And whenever Canadian sports fans ventured beyond our borders, they wrapped themselves in, or painted themselves with, Canadian flags.

One could safely argue, in fact, that the Canadian flag had become one of the world's most successful national symbols

Wayne and Shuster, English Canada's quintessential comedians and its most successful comic exports during the 1960s and 1970s, never missed a chance to poke fun at their country, as in their flag spoof (below).

Neither of them, however, was ever seen wearing a Canadian flag shoulder patch (right).

Joyce Wieland's *Confed-spread* (*below*) must rank as one of this patriotic artist's most patriotic pieces. Made in 1967, while Wieland was living in New York with her husband at the time, Michael Snow, it reflects the intense cultural nationalism that informs many of her works. In 1971, the National Gallery of Canada chose her for the first major show it ever dedicated to a living female Canadian artist. Naturally, the curators called it *True Patriot Love*.

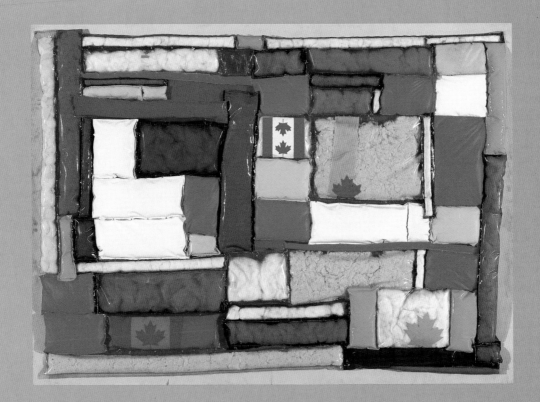

Plastic and cloth
146.2 cm x 200.4 cm

Charles Pachter's *The Painted Flag* (1981) is one of the more whimsical pieces in his ongoing flag series. One of his most recent flag paintings, created in the aftermath of September 11, 2001, shows the Maple Leaf and the American Stars and Stripes flying from a single pole.

Under the Black Flag (1971), by Christiane Pflug, belongs to a group of works the late Toronto artist painted either looking at or looking from the elementary school across the street from her studio. Several in this series include the school's Canadian flag. In this instance, the black of the flag combined with the heavy, dark treatment of the tree foliage gives the piece a very pessimistic feel. (The tiny green pennant beneath the Maple Leaf is the uniquely Canadian emblem of Elmer the Safety Elephant.)

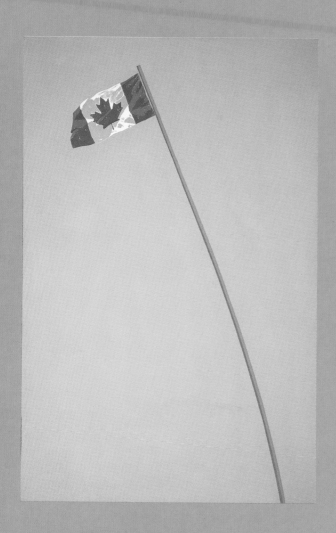

Acrylic on canvas
122 cm x 193 cm

Oil on canvas
137.2 cm x 142.2 cm

Since April 1939, when Trans-Canada Air Lines launched its passenger service with flights between Vancouver and Montreal, the airline has always flown under some version of the maple leaf. It changed its name to Air Canada in January 1965, just before the flag became official.

– instantly recognizable at home and abroad. The clarity of Jacques Saint-Cyr's maple leaf and the simplicity and readability of the flag's overall design had a lot to do with its easy acceptance. But the federal government did not simply sit back and wait for the Maple Leaf to imprint itself on the collective psyche. In the early 1970s, it began to deliberately craft a corporate identity around the country's attractive red-and-white standard. Inside or outside the country, the goal was for government departments and agencies and federal contributions to joint projects to be immediately recognized as Ottawa's.

Nowadays, whenever the word "Canada" is associated with the federal government, it most often appears with a cute Canadian flag flying from the "staff" of the *d*. This logo, known as the Canada wordmark, has become one of the world's most effective national brands. Canada's two other registered trademarks are its coat of arms and the flag symbol used in combination with the name of a government department or agency. These are the government's corporate signatures.

As the Maple Leaf rose to ever greater

heights in Canada and around the world, how did the new flag fly in the land of the fleur-de-lys? Was the burning of a flag in Montreal the day after the first flag raising an isolated act? In retrospect it looks more like a sign of things to come. By the time the flag was born, the people of la belle province had concerns other than a new Canadian flag on their minds: concerns like taking control of their economy and getting more respect within Confederation. The 1970s were the years of Quebec's first separatist government, which paved the way for the first referendum on sovereignty-association. These were years when relatively few Québécois saluted the Maple Leaf – even if it never stopped flying in front of Montreal City Hall or the legislature in Quebec City, the Assemblée nationale. (Quebec City would stop flying the Maple Leaf in front of its city hall in the late 1980s, but in April 1998 it returned to its rightful place "for reasons of convenience.")

Nonetheless, within little more than a decade after their flag was born, most Canadians at home and abroad had come to accept it without reservation. But the old flag – the Canadian Red Ensign – had not

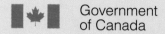 Government Gouvernment
of Canada du Canada

Canada

President Président
of the Treasury Board du Conseil du Trésor

IN 1969, the Official Languages Act was established to ensure the equality of French and English in all federal jurisdictions. That same year a task force reported that the government of Canada was projecting a confused and disorganized image to Canadians. The various symbols and identities used by government departments and government-funded organizations presented a hodge-podge of graphic and typographic elements, some employing the eleven-point maple leaf from the flag, some a quite different leaf and some no leaf at all. To create a stan-dardized and coherent "corporate identity" for the federal govern-ment, the government inaugurated its Federal Identity Program.

The creators of this identity quickly settled on its basic elements: a modified version of the Canadian flag, Canada's coat of arms and consistent use of government titles in both official languages. Helvetica was chosen as the official typeface – a clean, modern-looking face de-signed by Max Miedinger in 1957. Government institutions were to be identified by a "corporate signature" that was a combination of either the flag symbol or the coat of arms with their bilingual title.

In 1980, the Canada wordmark was added to the identity program as the government's global iden-tifier. Today the symbol marks Canada's presence wherever the government wants it to be known. In a sense, Canada's carefully crafted and assiduously guarded corporate identity is simply the latest step along an evolutionary road that began in medieval times when the first jousting knight placed a device on his armour to distinguish himself from his foe.

MAPLE LEAF MOTEL

NO VACANCY

INDOOR
SWIMING POOL
SPA & SAUNA

SENIORS DISCOUNT

NICE CLEAN ROOMS

If the maple leaf had long been a favourite motif for Canadian trademarks, its use exploded with the adoption of the new flag. Now Jacques Saint-Cyr's leaf became the proto-type for the majority of maple leaf logos, both commercial and govern-mental, as seen in this sampling. The leaf on the flag appears to be infin-itely adaptable, either as a trademark's primary design element or as an embellishment.

1 Canadian Snowboard Federation
2 Canadian Grain Commission
3 McDonald's Restaurants of Canada
4 Canadian Museum of Civilization

MARKS OF TRADE

1

2

3

4

These six trademarks have advertised some of Canada's most ubiquitous and successful enterprises, and each communicates its nationality by means of a maple leaf. The jersey worn by pre-war hockey star King Clancy (*bottom left*) has since been replaced with a blue knock-off of the new flag design. The Air Canada logo of 1973 (*top left*), designed not long after the new flag was born, clearly belongs to the same design family but doesn't have nearly the same presence.

1 Air Canada
2 Canadian Tire Corporation
3 Petro-Canada
4 Toronto Maple Leafs
5 Canadian National Railway Company
6 Greyhound Bus Lines

MAPLE LEAF MERCHANDISING

1

2

3

4

5

The Canadian Red Ensign obscures part of the national flag as RCMP pallbearers carry John Diefenbaker's coffin from the Parliament Buildings to Christ Church Cathedral, where the cortège was greeted by a nineteen-gun salute. The Chief's was by far the most elaborate state funeral ever accorded a Canadian leader. During his declining years he devoted much time to planning this final leave-taking, using as his model the state funeral of his hero, Sir Winston Churchill. Once the service concluded, the funeral party moved from the cathedral to the train station, where a carefully prepared funeral train awaited: three locomotives, the black-draped funeral car, five sleeping cars, a lounge car and a diner. "Two nights and three days across three provinces," wrote the *Globe and Mail*'s Joan Hollobon, one of the eighty-four passengers – journalists, old cronies and close family – who made the unprecedented land voyage. Thousands upon thousands of Canadians came out to watch the train pass to wave goodbye. And for that brief span all the man's flaws and failings were forgotten and he was again a "fighter for the underdog, an honest man sincere in his convictions and in his vision of Canada."

> "For all his virtues, the man himself could be vindictive and vengeful. He operated largely on intuition and had little consistent or coherent political philosophy. But he had a passionate idea and ideal of the country and he was a fervent if sometimes erratic nationalist."
>
> Journalist JOHN GRAY, writing on the occasion of Diefenbaker's state funeral

quite been properly laid to rest. The occasion for what appeared to be its final burial, appropriately enough, coincided with the death of its staunchest champion.

John Diefenbaker had lost the Tory leadership to Robert Stanfield in 1967 but refused to retire politely into the political night. In the spring of 1979, he fought and won his riding of Prince Albert, Saskatchewan, for the last time – living long enough to see his Tories returned to power under another westerner, Joe Clark, but not long enough to take his seat in the House. He died at his Ottawa home on August 16, 1979, a few weeks shy of his eighty-fourth birthday.

That evening his casket was placed in the Hall of Honour between the House of Commons and the Senate chamber, where he lay in state until Sunday, August 19, the day of his state funeral. But when the coffin emerged from the Centre Block on the shoulders of the eight scarlet-clad RCMP pallbearers who would carry it to Christ Church Cathedral, it was draped with two flags: the red-and-white Maple Leaf and the now-obsolete Red Ensign.

This bizarre compromise – the Red Ensign no longer carried even quasi-official status in Canada, except in the two versions flown as the provincial flags of Ontario and Manitoba – grew out of necessity: in order to get his state funeral Diefenbaker had to agree to have his coffin draped in the Maple Leaf flag. So, as his biographer Denis Smith reports in *Rogue Tory*, "at Diefenbaker's insistence, both the Red Ensign and the Canadian flag were draped on the coffin, the Red Ensign overlapping and obscuring the bottom of the maple leaf flag." At his funeral, Dief got the last laugh. But was it the Red Ensign's last hurrah?

BY FEBRUARY 1980, when Pierre Trudeau moved back into 24 Sussex Drive after making his remarkable return from the electoral dead, the new flag no longer looked all that new. It was now simply the Canadian flag, period, end of discussion – universally recognized and all but universally accepted as Canada's national emblem. However, as the prime minister reminded his fellow citizens soon after swearing in his cabinet, one final act of nation-building remained.

Canada's constitution – a British statute called the British North America Act – needed to be brought home, amended to

As Prime Minister Pierre Trudeau looks on, Queen Elizabeth II signs the official proclamation of the Constitution Act.

suit the complex federation the country had become and enacted by the Canadian House of Commons in both official languages. In the end Trudeau patriated the Constitution, but the full job of amending it is not yet done; he brought it to Canada by making a secret deal with most of the provinces and behind the backs of the delegation from Quebec, which deeply offended the government of the province whose pride of place in Confederation he had fought so long to assure.

Seventeen years after adopting the Maple Leaf flag, a deeply divided country once again took a highly symbolic step toward national unity. As George Stanley had pointed out in his March 1964 letter to John Matheson, the letter in which he sketched the flag design that formed the model for the Flag Committee's final choice, a flag is the simplest and most primitive way of expressing something as complicated as a country. To extend the thought: a constitution is a complicated way of expressing something as simple as one Canada, united by a set of laws and inalienable rights. And despite Quebec's anger over the way the Constitution came home, you would be hard-pressed today to find a citizen of

Quebec, anglophone or francophone, who would vote against the act's most important innovation, the Charter of Rights and Freedoms.

On a sunny, brisk Saturday, April 17, 1982, on a temporary stage set up in front of the Peace Tower near the spot where Lester Pearson and John Diefenbaker had witnessed the first official raising of the Maple Leaf, Elizabeth II, Queen of Canada, smiled as she signed the Constitution Act, 1982, into law. With the stroke of her regal pen the red-and-white flags that decorated every building on Parliament Hill took on a new meaning. Now those flags stood for a country that had at last embraced its status as an adult among the family of nations.

"When all is said and done, the Canadian federation presupposes that, over and above our respective neighbourhoods, towns, cities, and provinces, Canada is considered to be the homeland of all Canadians. To avoid making a clear choice as Canadians (rather than members of this or that province or city) by choosing to have feeble federal institutions would be to condemn ourselves to collective weakness in a world that will not be kind to nations divided against themselves.

A country, after all, is not something you build as the pharaohs built the pyramids, and then leave standing there to defy eternity. A country is something that is built every day out of certain basic shared values. And so it is in the hands of every Canadian to determine how well and wisely we shall build the country of the future."

PIERRE ELLIOTT TRUDEAU, *Memoirs*, 1993

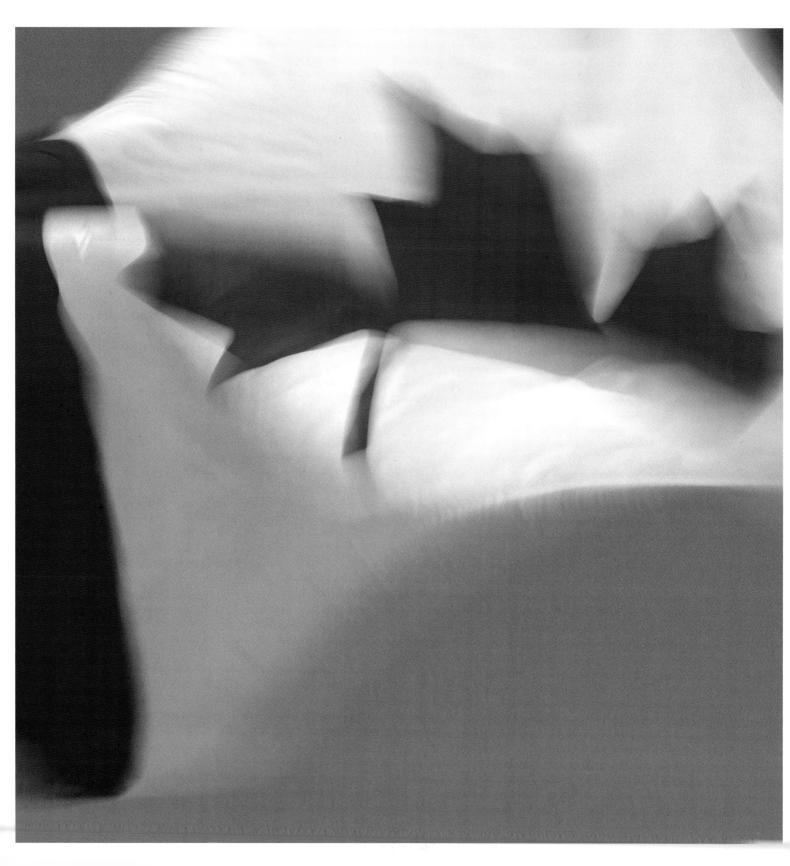

CHAPTER FIVE

A flag for the 21st century

THAT BLUSTERY SPRING DAY in 1982 when the Constitution Act became law marked a rite of passage for Canadians and their flag. It had taken the former British colony almost a hundred years after Confederation to mature into a country that could fly its own official banner. It took almost twenty years more before that country's constitution became an act of its own parliament. At long last, the Maple Leaf could proudly wave over a country that had achieved political independence, both in symbol and in fact.

But Canada still had a lot of growing up to do and in the next quarter century its flag would be brandished and buffeted in many ways. It would be waved high in victory, spat upon and burned in anger, raised in solidarity with its American cousins after the tragic events of September 11, 2001, flown from the summit of Mount Everest and lowered from every provincial flagpole in Newfoundland and Labrador by a premier angry with his treatment by Ottawa. It would shroud the coffin of Pierre Elliot Trudeau, our fifteenth prime minister, and lead the proud parade of our Olympic athletes at summer and winter games. Its original

versions would even become controversial relics as first one and then another "first flag" surfaced in the 1990s and the 2000s. And the country the Maple Leaf flew over would become, by the first decade of the twenty-first century, unrecognizable to the antagonists of the epic 1964 Flag Debate.

Yet even in a fresh century in a maturing country where the Maple Leaf flag had come to seem as inevitable as snow in winter, the ancient arguments could still erupt, including the long-ago controversy about the status of the Canadian Red Ensign. The trigger was a battle more venerable than the one waged by Lester Pearson and John Diefenbaker in the House of Commons: Vimy Ridge.

By the start of the twenty-first century, the magnificent Vimy Memorial in northern France was crumbling. This beautiful and haunting structure had been dedicated in 1936 to the more than 66,000 Canadians who died in Europe in World War I. It was inscribed with the names of the 11,285 soldiers killed in France whose resting places are unknown. After more than sixty years, water had eroded its limestone, concrete and masonry to the point where

Guy Viau, the Quebec member of the three-man panel that judged *Canadian Art*'s 1963 flag contest, summed up Canada's flag quest as well as any: "In my eyes, a Canadian flag must, first of all, indicate that we have cut the umbilical cord attaching us to the mother countries. A flag is not a genealogical tree or a history book ... It must be a simple design, recognizable at a distance, a bright clear note in the sky. A balanced and harmonious composition which will carry its meaning unfolding or fluttering in the wind."

King Edward VIII unveiled Canada's towering Vimy Memorial at the July 1936 dedication ceremonies, which were attended by fifty thousand veterans and their families along with representatives of all three services in the Canadian Armed Forces. Here a contingent from the Canadian Navy marches past the reviewing party. The memorial, designed by Canadian sculptor Walter Allward, cost $1.5 million and took eleven years to build. By the time of its dedication, a second great war loomed.

many of the names were no longer readable. In 2004, as the capstone of a major plan to refurbish all of Canada's world war memorials, the Department of Veterans Affairs commissioned restoration work that included re-carving the names and restoring the monumental statues. In the spring of 2007, on the ninetieth anniversary of the Battle of Vimy Ridge, the monument would be officially rededicated in a ceremony presided over by Queen Elizabeth II and the French and Canadian prime ministers and attended by many dignitaries and veterans.

One would think such an event would provide an ideal moment to bring Canadians together, an opportunity to honour the past while celebrating the immense progress the country has made since it fought in a world-altering war without a flag to call its own. Instead, the weeks leading up to the April 9 rededication were filled with the sound of an increasingly vocal campaign to fly the Canadian Red Ensign at Vimy, the flag that had supposedly been permanently discharged from active duty on February 15, 1965. Fittingly, the campaign was led by veterans groups, chief among them the Royal Canadian Legion, which back in 1964 had spearheaded the resistance to the Pearson Pennant and promoted the Canadian Red Ensign as the only choice for the official national flag of Canada.

The Legion's argument in 2007 was simple: The Red Ensign should fly alongside the Maple Leaf at the Vimy ceremony because it was the flag our soldiers "fought and died under" during the First World War. Never mind that the Red Ensign was never Canada's official flag, in war or in peace. Like a recessive genetic trait that skips a generation or two, the Red Ensign was once again front and centre. A few objected, most prominently retired General Roméo Dallaire, who argued that "to put the Red Ensign at the same level as the French and current Canadian flag is absolutely against all possible protocol." But the Legion lobbied hard and even managed to persuade the two surviving veterans of the Great War to sign their names to letters urging the prime minister to acquiesce. The campaign went further, arguing that the Canadian ensign should fly at Vimy in perpetuity.

UNTIL RECENTLY, most Canadians knew nothing of the Canadian Red Ensign that had been donated to the Imperial War Museum in London in 1918 by Lieutenant-Colonel Lorn Paulet Owen Tudor, commander of the 5th Canadian Infantry Battalion. Apparently, Tudor brought the flag with him from Canada and carried it into the battles of Vimy Ridge, Lens, Hill 70 and Passchendaele. But it is the flag's association with Vimy that gives it special status. Before its recent restoration, age and wear accounted for its considerable deterioration – not battle damage. (No sane soldier would have waved a red flag while advancing on the German trenches!) Most likely, Colonel Tudor kept the flag neatly folded in his rucksack as a patriotic keepsake.

Over the years, the London museum refused several requests for the flag's repatriation on the grounds that its holdings were intended to represent the whole British Empire, not simply Great Britain. After Duane Daly, Dominion Secretary of the Royal Canadian Legion, made the return of the Vimy Ensign his personal cause, the British finally agreed to lend this priceless historical artifact to Canada in time for the May 2005 opening of the Canadian War Museum in Ottawa. For the next two years it greeted visitors about to enter the museum's permanent galleries. The ensign was returned to the Imperial War Museum in 2008.

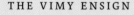

THE VIMY ENSIGN

This photograph is as close as most Canadians will get to the Vimy Ensign. Major restoration work in 2005 has made the wear and tear of its ninety-plus years scarcely discernible. If you look closely, you'll see that the flag consists of multiple pieces of cloth. The Union Jack in the upper hoist is a patchwork of red, white and blue wool while the shield in the fly is a single piece of printed cloth; both are machine-stitched to the main flag made of red wool bunting. (The obverse of the ensign is blank – proof it was never meant to be flown.) At the top of the canvas sleeve along the hoist is a wooden toggle attached to a cord. The manufacturer's name printed on the canvas has faded beyond legibility, but you can still read the stamp "CANADA."

One of the virtues of the Maple Leaf flag's design is that it's easy to tell top from bottom. But accidents happen, as fans of the Toronto Blue Jays vividly remember. Just before Game 2 of the 1992 World Series between Toronto and Atlanta, a colour guard of U.S. Marines (*left*) marched onto Atlanta's Grant Field flying the Canadian flag upside-down. The colour guard travelled to Toronto for Game 3 and rectified their error, but a group of SkyDome fans got in the last word. They displayed a banner broadcasting the words "No Hard Feelings," with the words upside-down.

More embarrassing was the gaffe committed on Parliament Hill during Canada Day ceremonies on July 1, 1999. Governor General Roméo LeBlanc (*below*) must have been less than amused when his own Governor General's Foot Guards marched past him flying an upside-down Maple Leaf.

The Conservative government listened. And on March 30, 2007, the Secretary of State for Multicultural and Canadian Identity, Jason Kenney, announced that the Red Ensign would be a permanent feature of the Vimy Memorial. "You sort of wonder sometimes," Dallaire commented, "at the maturity of our nation in things of this nature." But maybe the lack of fuss over the Red Ensign's comeback was actually a sign of maturity. By 2007, the Maple Leaf flag, Canada's first and only official national flag, had become so embedded in the national psyche that giving a formal nod to Sir John A.'s "old flag" seemed only right and proper.

To bring the Red Ensign out of retirement, Kenney referred the matter to the Canadian Heraldic Authority, which since its establishment in 1988 has been responsible for granting or approving all armorial bearings, including flags. The authority concluded that the ensign ought to be entered into the Public Register of Arms, Flags and Badges of Canada. Thus the flag that flew from government buildings and Canadian embassies between 1957 and 1965 at last achieved recognition as an official national symbol.

On April 9, the Maple Leaf flag fluttered in glorious spring sunshine, flanked by the Red Ensign and the French tricolour, as a mostly Canadian crowd estimated at more than twenty thousand gathered in the natural amphitheatre at the foot of the Vimy monument. Their numbers included many descendants of the men who'd fought at the battle and many ordinary Canadians. The prime ministers spoke movingly of honour and sacrifice, but the highlight of the proceedings came with the arrival of several thousand Canadian high school students, each dressed in a replica World War I uniform and each wearing the name of a soldier who had died in the battle. One prominent Canadian politician present called it "one of the best days to be a Canadian I can remember."

It was also a sad ceremony, made sadder by the knowledge that only the day before a roadside bomb in southern Afghanistan had killed six members of the Royal Canadian Regiment, a regiment whose members had distinguished themselves at the Battle of Vimy Ridge and paid the price. It was the worst single-day Canadian loss of the Afghan war and brought the military death

Appropriately, the ensign raised at the Vimy Memorial for its 2007 rededication was a replica of the Vimy Ensign, but the decision to fly this particular version was reached only after some debate among those concerned with flag protocol. By 1917, Canada had grown to include nine provinces, yet the Vimy Ensign is a four-province version dating back to 1868, when only Ontario, Quebec, Nova Scotia and New Brunswick had joined Confederation. That this out-of-date ensign was still in use long after it had become technically obsolete is further evidence of the gap between theory and practice in the evolution of Canada's unofficial national standard.

Pallbearers carry the casket of Corporal Matthew McCully during a repatriation ceremony at CFB Trenton on Monday, May 28, 2007. The forty-fourth soldier killed in Afghanistan, McCully was the victim of a roadside bomb.

toll to fifty-two. Appropriately, the Queen concluded her speech (delivered in both English and French) with these words: "To those who have so recently lost their lives in Afghanistan, to Canada and to all who would serve the cause of freedom, I rededicate this magnificently restored memorial."

On the day the Queen spoke the war in Afghanistan was already five and a half years old. The joint U.S.-British invasion had begun with air strikes on October 7, 2001, a few weeks after the terrorist attacks on the World Trade Center and the Pentagon. By the end of the year, Afghanistan's main population centres had fallen under U.S. and British control and the Taliban and their al Qaeda allies were defeated militarily. But bringing peace to Afghanistan would prove a far tougher mission. By early 2003, the Taliban's surviving forces had regrouped and launched the insurgency that continues to this day.

Afghanistan has highlighted certain Canadian military virtues that have reminded many of Vimy. Like their World War I counterparts, Canadian soldiers in Kandahar have become known for staying calm under fire and for doing the job without boasting. As they did at Vimy, they take on the toughest tasks. When they make mistakes, they admit them and move on. And, as in World War I, their country has been fighting well above its population weight. Canada's long tradition of military sacrifice continues.

As well as being a source of both national pride and political controversy, the return of Canadian soldiers to active combat has marked a new development in the life story of our flag. For the first time in our history, Canadian troops have been fighting under the Maple Leaf, thereby completing a narrative that began at least as far back as 1884, when a volunteer Canadian contingent of lumberjacks and voyageurs commanded by a Toronto alderman travelled to Sudan to join a force dispatched to rescue General Charles Gordon from the besieged city of Khartoum.

As the Afghan war has worn on, the steadily mounting number of Canadian deaths has placed the Canadian Armed Forces in a spotlight they haven't known since the Korean War and caused Canadians at home to ask themselves how they

FROM FAILING HANDS

As the Peace Tower flag flies at half-mast on April 18, 2002, sculpted figures of World War I soldiers on the National War Memorial in Ottawa seem to mourn the Canadians killed in Afghanistan that day.

SOON AFTER the Conservatives took power in the spring of 2006, Prime Minister Stephen Harper announced that the media would be barred from repatriation ceremonies for fallen soldiers out of respect for the privacy of grieving families. His announcement was met with widespread opposition, especially from bereaved military families, who said they welcomed public participation in their mourning process. A few weeks later, the policy was reversed. But the issue of how to properly and equitably honour soldiers killed in combat remains.

Only since 1970 has it been standard practice to bring home the bodies of the fallen for burial in Canada. In both world wars and for long before, the dead were buried "where they fell." (In major twentieth-century conflicts, the number of losses would have made repatriation impractical.)

What, then, should be the policy for half-masting the Maple Leaf that flies from the Peace Tower? A royal decree of 1919 (prompted by the enormous loss of Canadian lives in World War I) left the lowering of the Peace Tower flag to the discretion of the government of the day. But only in 2002, with the first Afghan fatalities, did the Liberal government begin half-masting the flag each time a soldier died, a policy rescinded by the newly elected Conservatives to considerable public outcry.

In the spring of 2008, a special flag advisory committee recommended that once a year, on Remembrance Day, all fallen soldiers in war and peacekeeping be honoured by half-masting the Peace Tower flag. The committee also recommended that the existing practice of lowering the flag on "special days," including those remembering police officers who died in the line of duty, be abolished. Robert Watt, Canada's former chief herald who chaired the committee, explained: "We wanted to reinforce [half masting's] importance by focusing it in as precise and clear a way as possible." Most veterans groups supported the committee, but the groups whose flag privileges would be revoked were outraged.

wish to project their country's power and image in the twenty-first century. Since the 1956 Suez crisis, the reputation of Canadian soldiers has been primarily that of peacekeepers. On peacekeeping missions, our national flag is worn as a shoulder patch and takes second place to the flag of the United Nations. Since the First Gulf War of 1991, however, when Canada joined the UN-sanctioned coalition that liberated Kuwait from Iraqi occupation, Canada's modern military image has begun to change. In that war, Canadian forces provided modest naval, air and logistical support. Our soldiers – including the first Canadian female soldiers to serve in a combat zone – operated in a military, not a peacekeeping capacity.

In a world where the combatants so seldom represent distinct national entities, peacekeeping has become increasingly difficult. In Somalia, in Yugoslavia, and in Rwanda, Canadian peacekeepers have watched more or less helplessly while warring factions have committed atrocities ranging from the Rwandan genocide of 1994 to the ethnic cleansing perpetrated by Serb forces at Srebrenica in 1995. More

and more, the international community seems to be moving away from traditional peacekeeping and toward a more activist role under either NATO or the United Nations. As an example of this, Canada joined the NATO-backed war in Afghanistan in 2001 but did not join the U.S.-led invasion of Iraq in 2003 on the grounds that it was not sanctioned by the UN. And since arriving in Afghanistan, Canada's soldiers have been engaged in decidedly active military duties. So it is legitimate to ask whether our long-cherished role as international peacekeepers is being abandoned and if we will soon see a day when the world ceases to view the eleven-pointed maple leaf as a symbol of the peaceful resolution of potentially deadly conflict.

Whatever the future of international peacekeeping, at home Canada's flag will continue to fly over one of the most polyglot nations on earth, a veritable United Nations of colours, cultures and languages. This multicultural miracle – for that is truly what it is – would have been unimaginable in a country represented by a flag adorned with symbols bequeathed by its original European colonizers: the fleur-

de-lys and the Union Jack. I would argue, in fact, that the Maple Leaf has truly come into its own as a national symbol only since the Charter of Rights and Freedoms came into effect and balanced Canada's historic emphasis on collective rights with strong protection of individual rights.

Ironically, given that Quebec did not endorse the 1982 Constitution, the Charter entrenched by Trudeau is now as popular in La Belle Province as anywhere in the country – while public opinion surveys have repeatedly confirmed that Canadians value it almost as much as universal health care. Some have argued that until Quebec is finally brought into the "constitutional family" the country's survival is at risk. And it is true that in the quarter century since patriation Canada has experienced some serious stresses and survived one near-death experience, the 1995 Quebec referendum.

During the weeks leading up to the October 30 sovereignty vote, public opinion polls consistently showed the pro-sovereigntist "Yes" side with the edge. In both camps there was a great deal of flag-waving, almost as if the local sugar maple leaf and

Until recently, Canadian soldiers were known less for waging war than for keeping the peace. In March 2001, Major Mike Voith, commanding officer of the 4th Engineer Support Regiment, pin-ned the Canadian Peace-keeping Service Medal on three Canadian peace-keepers (*bottom*), including Sapper Eugene Spencer and Sapper Amanda Perry (*foreground*), who had served for more than one hundred days as part of the United Nations Mission in Ethiopia and Eritrea. The medal recognizes peace-keeping service by Cana-dians deployed outside of Canada for a minimum period of thirty days.

Peacekeeping is often dangerous work, as it proved for Corporal Mark Isfeld, who died in Croatia in 1994 while removing land mines. Two peace-keepers (*below left*), Master Corporal Perry Collins (*at left*) and Sapper David McCormick, distributed "Izzy" dolls named in Isfeld's memory to Eritrean children on May 25, 2001.

ANY CITIZEN OF CANADA can be appointed to the Order of Canada, the country's highest civilian honour, and nominations can be made by individuals or groups. There are roughly eight hundred nominations per year and there have been more than five thousand recipients since Governor General Roland Michener presented the first medals on July 1, 1967. The medal design is a stylized snowflake with Jacques Saint-Cyr's maple leaf in the centre. The Order's motto, *Desiderantes Meliorem Patriam* (They Desire a Better Country) encircles the maple leaf.

In any year there can be no more than 220 appointments, including a maximum of 15 appointments to the highest level, Companion of the Order. And at any given time there can be no more than 165 living Companions.

In the words of John Matheson, one of the first to urge Mike Pearson to make a civilian honours system a reality, "the Order was conceived and developed in the fragrant memory of one who believed each life is unique and irreplaceable … Prime Minister Pearson, who shunned all pretensions to righteousness, shared this optimism that man at heart is good, and that life is a series of opportunities wherein we may correct error, learn from mistakes and progress to something better."

THEY DESIRE A BETTER COUNTRY

Companion of the
Order of Canada

Officer of the
Order of Canada

Member of the
Order of Canada

the foreign French lily were duking it out for the allegiance of *les Québécois.* In the end, the "No" side won by the narrowest of margins. But surely the most powerful image from the period remains the sea of Quebec and Canadian flags that joined together in the massive federalist rally held in Montreal one week before the vote.

In the years since the referendum, support in Quebec for "sovereignty," whatever the word might mean in practice, has remained high, while the actual prospect of separation has seemed more and more remote. The fiery young nationalists of the Quiet Revolution of the 1960s have grown older and their province has gained much of the autonomy they earlier dreamed of but without Quebec leaving Confederation. The province's recent prosperity hasn't hurt either. But arguably, the deciding factor has been the demographic shift resulting from successive waves of immigrants to Canada who have settled in Quebec.

Among those new Québécois was a teenage Michaëlle Jean, who arrived in Canada from Haiti in 1968. Almost forty years later, on September 27, 2005, Mme Jean was installed as Canada's twenty-seventh governor general. In her installation speech she spoke of a new Canadian reality. "The time of the 'two solitudes' that for too long described the character of this country is past," she said. Jean then expanded on the traditional definition in very twenty-first century terms. "The narrow notion of 'every person for himself' does not belong in today's world, which demands that we learn to see beyond our wounds, beyond our differences for the good of all … we must eliminate the spectre of all the solitudes and promote solidarity among all the citizens who make up the Canada of today." Coming from a French-speaking, Haitian-born, Québécoise of African origin, these words carried the weight of first-hand experience and the spirit of a Quebec completely different from the place where a child by the name of Pierre Elliott Trudeau was born in October 1919.

The Quebec Trudeau knew for the first half of his life was divided between an English-speaking solitude with a monopoly on economic power and a French-speaking solitude dominated by a deeply reactionary Catholic church. By the time of Trudeau's death at the age of eighty-two in late

The big unity rally in Montreal on October 27, 1995, wasn't the only public demonstration of support for the federalist cause as the Quebec referendum loomed. Thousands of Nova Scotians attended this Halifax rally, one of many held across the country that day. Another cheerful crowd had gathered on Parliament Hill the previous February 15, when Prime Minister Jean Chrétien presided over Canada's first official National Flag of Canada Day. At the unity rallies, however, there were as many *fleurdelisé* flags as Maple Leafs. And the message all those people with all their flags were trying to send was simple: "My Canada includes Quebec."

September 2001, Quebec and Canada had changed profoundly and his part in those changes had made him into a rare kind of Canadian icon, as demonstrated by the public response to his passing.

On October 1 and 2, 2000, sixty thousand people, many of them carrying Trudeau's signature red rose, filed past the Maple-Leaf-flag-draped coffin as his body lay in state in the Hall of Honour on Parliament Hill. But the most striking display of public affection occurred on October 3 when thousands upon thousands of people came out on an unseasonably fine fall day to watch the train bearing Trudeau's coffin travel from Ottawa to Montreal and his state funeral at Montreal's Notre-Dame Basilica. And it is this public expression of grief rather than the official rites in Ottawa and Montreal that will be remembered. Many of the track-side onlookers flew Canadian flags from makeshift flag-staffs, including at least one hockey stick. One woman waved a handmade cherry paddle, a reference to Trudeau's great love of canoeing. Countless others made similar gestures during this unprecedented outpouring of grief and patriotism.

Happily, the Maple Leaf flag has been raised more often in celebration than in sorrow during the last twenty-five years. Consider the explosion of flags that followed the second of two gold medals won by the women's and men's hockey teams at the 2002 Salt Lake City Winter Olympics. There was a lot to cheer about: For the first time in fifty years Canada had won an Olympic gold medal in hockey and for the first time ever it had captured two hockey golds at a single Games.

Seconds after the final buzzer of the men's game sounded on February 24, the main streets of Canada began to fill with cars and motorcycles and with thousands upon thousands of flag-wavers. In the country's largest cities, the crowds made up a heady mix of Canadians of all ages and origins, many of them born in countries where ice is as rare as diamonds and the game of ice hockey is a childhood fairy tale. These strangers were high-fiving and shaking hands with each other, even hugging. There was an incredible sweetness in the air. For a few hours on that Sunday afternoon and evening, the main streets of Canada morphed into one long Main

On October 3, 2000, the state funeral of Pierre Elliott Trudeau took place in Montreal's Notre-Dame Basilica (*left*), where the three thousand mourners included Cuban President Fidel Castro, former U.S. president Jimmy Carter, and the Aga Kahn. The day before, Bob Joiner (*below*) of Limoges, Ontario, was one of the many who turned out to watch the passage of Trudeau's funeral train. Few remained indifferent to the death of Canada's most colourful prime minister since Sir John A. Macdonald.

In April 2001, astronaut Chris Hadfield (*below*) became the first Canadian to walk in space. Once floating weightless outside the space shuttle, his job was to unwrap what he called "a huge present," the Canadarm 2, which had been carried in the cargo bay of *Endeavour* (*left*) to its successful rendezvous with the International Space Station. Hadfield completed his mission successfully; the fifty-seven-foot-long, Canadian-designed-and-built Space Station Remote Manipulator System would help complete construction of the space outpost and play an essential role in maintaining it.

Street that stretched from coast to coast to coast, a red-white-red line that connected Canadians in some profound yet joyous way, bridging solitudes without denying differences.

Perhaps even more revealing than this hockey euphoria – hockey being about as close as we come to having a national religion – was the response to the games of the 2006 soccer World Cup in Germany. In downtown Toronto and other urban centres across the land, each and every game was followed by enthusiastic celebrations. No matter which country had won the game that day, honking cars with flag-waving occupants suddenly materialized to trumpet a victory by Brazil or South Korea or Poland or Mexico or Ghana. And along with the national flag of the victorious country, almost every vehicle also flew a red-white-red Maple Leaf. Following the final match, a nail-biter that Italy finally won over France on a penalty shoot-out after the end of extra time, the Canadian flag seemed temporarily overlaid with the Italian flag's vertical bars of green, white and red.

Of course we expect people to wave the flag after a sporting victory. More telling is

when they wave it in times of crisis. And surely one of our flag's finest hours since the start of the twenty-first century came in the immediate aftermath of 9/11. Throughout the country in the days that followed, the Maple Leaf and the Stars and Stripes were flown side by side in sorrow and solidarity with our American cousins. As Pierre Trudeau once famously observed, it can be uncomfortable sharing the North American bed with the U.S. elephant. And our history is marked by a series of episodes of anti-Americanism that are byproducts of both proximity and family feeling. All families have their spats, but when the chips are down, Canadians and Americans have always recognized their family bond.

Undoubtedly the subsequent U.S.-led invasion and occupation of Iraq has tested that bond. The efforts of our police, border and intelligence services to meet American demands to increase border security and root out potential terrorist elements on Canadian soil have led to the first serious erosion of human rights enshrined in Trudeau's Charter. Commissions of enquiry have found our security services complicit in the incarceration without charges and

Hockey fans Jamie Hyslop (*left*) and Tracey Rai painted themselves with the flag before making the trek from Delta, British Columbia, to join the crowd gathered at GM Place arena to watch Team Canada beat the Americans at the Salt Lake City Olympics. (Rai is also wearing a tuque shaped like a maple leaf.) The victory celebrations in downtown Vancouver lasted into the wee hours of Monday morning.

Canada's Olympic hockey euphoria was launched when the women's team, led by Hayley Wickenheiser (*right*), upset the highly favoured United States team, 3 to 2. Their on-ice heroics seemed to inspire the men's team, which had to battle hard before prevailing over Team USA by a score of 5 to 2. Canada's twin hockey golds in February 2002 triggered a coast-to-coast orgy of flag-waving. In Salt Lake City, Utah, Captain Mario Lemieux (*above*) did some flag-waving of his own as he celebrated Team Canada's victory. Amazingly, it was the first Olympic gold for a Canadian men's hockey team since the Edmonton Mercurys, an amateur outfit sponsored by an Edmonton car dealership, had beaten an American team in 1952.

To some the Maple Leaf does not always stand for peace, order and good government. This Serbian, for example, was demonstrating in Ottawa on March 27, 1999, against NATO air strikes in Yugoslavia. A couple of years later, a group of protesters from Topeka, Kansas, burned what they called Canada's "Fag Flag" in front of the Supreme Court building after the Canadian high court ruled in favour of granting spousal benefits to same-sex partners working under federal jurisdiction. On a far more positive note, hundreds of thousands of Canadians expressed solidarity with their American neighbours following the tragic events of September 11, 2001, by flying their two countries' flags side by side in countless demonstrations both large and small, like this massive rally held on Parliament Hill on the international day of mourning for all who had died in the terrorist attacks (*opposite*).

torture abroad of several Canadian citizens. But those who worry that Canadian democracy isn't strong enough to survive these recent challenges need only look at the kind of country Canada's flag has come to stand for.

A flag in and of itself has no meaning until the people who have chosen it give it meaning. Otherwise it remains merely a scrap of fabric or, in then-Quebec-premier Bernard Landry's unfortunate phrase, "un morceau de chiffon rouge," a piece of red rag. A flag can truly be said to mean something when it is taken seriously enough to be carried into battle, raised in celebration or lowered in protest, as it was by Newfoundland and Labrador premier Danny Williams on December 23, 2004, in retaliation for Ottawa's stand on the sharing of royalties from offshore oil and gas. Williams wanted 100 percent of the royalties for his province; Prime Minister Paul Martin refused. "They're slapping us in the face," Williams said. "I'm not willing to fly that flag anymore in the province." The subject of this typical federal-provincial tiff isn't the point. The point is that the Maple Leaf seemed worth lowering in the

first place. A few weeks later Williams ran it up the flagpole again. "The statement has been made," he told reporters, "and now we will be raising the flag as proud Canadians."

As Williams's actions demonstrated, symbols matter. They matter to politicians and to ordinary citizens. In the fall of 2007, the newly elected Saskatchewan government announced it was considering replacing the three golden sheaves of wheat on the provincial shield. "We want the visual identity of Saskatchewan to be something more modern that depicts what we are all about," opined Saskatchewan deputy premier Ken Krawetz. Easier said than done. Public response was so overwhelmingly negative that the government shelved the idea. In all likelihood, recent talk of replacing the Manitoba bison or the wild rose of Alberta won't get very far either. But such rumblings do indicate a desire by Canadian governments to project a different, more contemporary image to the world. The most notable recent example of this trend was undertaken in 2007 by the Canadian Tourism Commission (CTC), the federal marketing organization

"A century from now, historians and anthropologists will cite Canada as a harbinger of a new age. The new age will be marked by a steep reduction in intolerances so deeply ingrained in human culture that for millennia we have shaped our caste systems and fought our wars based on them."

JOHN IBBITSON

that works to persuade foreign tourists to visit Canada.

Twenty-first century Canada is about as far removed as imaginable from the medieval world that gave birth to the first heraldic emblems, which eventually evolved into crests, coats of arms and national flags. But the ancient desire to find the apt image to represent an essential identity undoubtedly lives on in the current preoccupation with branding. Few corporate and government entities have not put themselves through an exhaustive process of rebranding, of rethinking and refining the message they want to communicate, then developing words and images that encapsulate this message. In these terms, Canada's first modern branding exercise was the choosing of the Maple Leaf flag in 1964.

Traditionally the CTC has exploited the stereotypical view of Canada as the country of moose, mountains, and Mounties, a vast, sparsely populated land offering spectacular scenery and wide open spaces. The CTC's rebranding exercise yielded a new marketing slogan, "Explorez sans fin / Keep Exploring," and a new visual identity that, not surprisingly, centred on the "simple and welcoming image of the maple leaf." The CTC leaf, meant to project a friendly informality, nonetheless owes its essence to Jacques Saint-Cyr's iconic original, right down to its eleven points.

Indeed, one of the great virtues of the maple leaf symbol has been its adaptability. And the single, many-pointed leaf has now grown to encompass the essence of twenty-first century Canada, a place that has welcomed – and continues to welcome – so many people from so many different parts of the world. The sheer variety of cultures and perspectives Canada contains has become the essential stuff of its identity. Moreover, in a country where the birth rate has fallen below the population-replacement rate, immigrants now account for all of Canada's population growth and, crucially, for the growth in the labour force on which its economic prosperity depends. With every passing year, Canada becomes more and more a country of immigrants and the children of immigrants. Just as inevitably, all these newcomers see their adopted country and the flag that flies over it with fresh eyes.

One of the most interesting findings from recent censuses is the number of

explorez sans fin
Canada
keep exploring

people who identify their ethnic origin as Canadian. In 2006, these numbered more than ten million, almost a third of the total population of thirty-three million, and, of these, nearly six million defined their ethnic identity as Canadian and nothing else. These "ethnic" Canadians are evidence of a widespread and unprecedented cultural mixing in which distinct cultural groups with different customs and beliefs interact with and enrich each other while inexorably altering mainstream society. Another striking indication of the unique nature of Canada's emerging socio-cultural potpourri is the number of couples where one partner is identified as belonging to a visible minority and the other is not. The 2006 census reported a quarter of a million such "mixed" unions.

Observant outsiders will tell you that the Maple Leaf flag now stands for the very diversity that Canadians – old-stock and new – are only beginning to grasp. The Aga Khan, spiritual leader of the world's more than fifteen million Ismaili Muslims, describes Canada as "the most successful pluralist society on the face of the globe... an amazing global asset." In partnership with the federal government, the Aga Khan has established the Global Centre for Pluralism in Ottawa. Appropriately located in the building formerly housing the Canadian War Museum, the centre aims to promote "the values, practices and policies that underpin pluralist societies" by "drawing inspiration from the Canadian experience."

Among professional historians and educators, there has been much hand-wringing over Canadians' ignorance of their history. But the history they worry about won't mean much if it isn't understood in terms of the country's demographic sea-change. And perhaps some healthy historical revisionism is already occurring as Canada begins the process of rewriting its foundation myth – the shared story a country's people tell to explain their country to themselves and to the world. For a long time, Canada's foundation myth told of two European peoples who forged a workable union despite the violent conquest of one by the other. This was the myth enshrined in official bilingualism and played out during a succession of unity crises dating back to the early days of

According to the Canadian Tourism Commission, its new visual identity is "the first bold step toward re-imaging Canada's position as a global destination brand." The CTC sees its new logo as "a contemporary take on this national icon" and believes "Our powerful Canada: Keep Exploring visual identity will anchor our communications across all media." As well as the bilingual version seen here, the logo is available in English, French and Spanish.

During Canada Day celebrations on Parliament Hill on July 1, 2005, Prime Minister Paul Martin holds high the most recent contender for "first" flag honours. While this flag was the first to be hoisted atop the Peace Tower on February 15, 1965, it certainly wasn't the first Maple Leaf raised on that historic day. Out of the government's initial mass-produced order of forty thousand, a total of twelve thousand flags were ready by the date of the official flag-raising ceremony, each of them physically indistinguishable from the other. But it's unlikely the Peace Tower flag will be discredited, in contrast to the previous first flag contender. In February 2000 the chair of the Liberal caucus produced a flag he believed had been raised first and then given to the caucus by Lester Pearson. At a hastily called news conference (opposite) Prime Minister Jean Chrétien and Heritage Minister Sheila Copps trumpeted the historic discovery and vowed that it would be properly displayed. The recently completed Canadian Museum of Civilization announced plans to put the flag on display – until it turned out to be a fake.

THE FIRST FLAG MYSTERY

THE SENTIMENTAL VALUE placed on the souvenir of a defining moment defies logic. The puck that scores the winning goal in the Stanley Cup final is nothing more than a black rubber disk like countless others, but we cherish it nonetheless. So it's no surprise that the first Maple Leaf flag officially flown on February 15, 1965, remains an object of great interest, especially since no one seems to know what happened to it.

Before the new flag was raised, Pearson's cabinet met and decided "it was important that the Red Ensign lowered at the ceremony, the new flag there raised and other historic items relevant to the creation of a new flag be sent to the Archives or to the Canadian Historical Museum for safekeeping and display." But after the ceremony was over the Maple Leaf flag vanished.

Not that there haven't been claimants. On February 15, 2000, the chair of the national Liberal caucus presented Heritage Minister Sheila Copps with what

he believed was the first flag, but experts at the Canadian Conservation Institute subsequently discovered a stamp on the fabric that indicated the caucus flag came from a later production run, so could not be the very first one.

In the spring of 2006, a far more serious claimant came forward when the widow of Lucien Lamoureux, Deputy Speaker of the House of Commons during the 1964 Flag Debate, gave back to Canada the flag that had draped her husband's coffin. This proved to be the first Maple Leaf flown from the Peace Tower, a significant memento certainly, but definitely not the first new flag flown that day. Protocol requires that the governor general's personal standard wave from the Peace Tower flagstaff whenever the Crown's representative is on Parliament Hill. On that day of flag-related ceremonies, the new flag could be raised from the tower only after Governor General Georges Vanier returned to Rideau Hall, by which time every other official flagpole

in Ottawa already had a Maple Leaf flapping in the February sun.

Possible clues to the first flag's whereabouts can be found in the records of the Privy Council Office and in the archives of the Canadian Museum of Civilization (CMC). These indicate that various items connected to both the Pearson Pennant and the Maple Leaf, including flag models and designs and possibly the first flag (although there is no specific mention of this), were transferred to the Human History Branch, National Museum of Canada (now part of the CMC) on July 19, 1966, and that the museum's director, Dr. Richard Glover, acknowledged receipt. None of the material has since been found. In 2000, the Museum of Civilization launched an exhaustive and unsuccessful search for the missing trove of flag treasure. And there the mystery rests.

The Canadian Heraldic Authority's (CHA) coat of arms exemplifies the modern art of heraldry. Although the elements haven't changed since the Middle Ages, heraldic language has been adapted and new symbolism invented. Here the shield's supporters are mythic creatures, half raven, half polar bear. The red maple leaf in the centre of the shield is charged with a smaller shield, representing the authority's responsibility to create new arms. Any Canadian citizen or institution may petition the Chief Herald of Canada to grant new arms, a badge or a flag. To qualify, petitioners must have made contribution to their communities. Once an individual's petition is approved, one of the CHA's heralds helps develop the petitioner's personal escutcheon.

Confederation, and which probably reached their peak during the October Crisis of 1970. The inadequacies of the old story have long been apparent, not least in the story's failure to mention Canada's First Nations. This traditional narrative barely begins to account for what Canada has become and is in the process of becoming.

The new story that we will be telling our children long after the last veteran of Vimy has passed from memory goes something like this: Canada has always been an experiment in the accommodation of differences, always a country searching for ways that traditional antagonists and former strangers can live peaceably and profitably together. For much of our history, this has meant a delicate political dance between the so-called solitudes of English and French Canada, a dance that pretty much ignored everyone else. But for all its limitations, the post-Confederation dance taught us how to invite strangers onto the dance floor. The twenty-first-century Canadian dance is trickier and we're still learning all the steps. It involves multiple partners and pairings that shift often. It's a dance where the beat can change in an instant. But we're starting to realize just how original it is.

To drop the metaphor and restate the point, we've nurtured a society in which pluralism – the richness and variety inherent in cultural diversity – is the primary shared value. That's what our flag stands for above all its other meanings: a singularity that miraculously emerges out of multiplicity, a unity that affirms diversity.

WHEN THE HOUSE OF COMMONS in Ottawa convened on the afternoon of Thursday, October 29, 1964, Alan Beddoe sat in the Visitors' Gallery and listened as Herman Batten, the Newfoundland Liberal who chaired the joint-party Flag Committee, rose from his seat on the government side to deliver the committee's final report. No individual had contributed more than Beddoe to the deliberations of the committee. As its appointed heraldic expert he had instructed committee members on the fine points of flags and emblems. As its design consultant he had sketched and painted endless options and executed the paintings of the fifteen finalists the committee voted on. But he didn't yet know the winner. Beddoe listened intently as Batten informed the House that the committee was recommending a flag that would bear a single red maple leaf.

In his diary, Beddoe wrote that he left the House "in utter disgust and despair" at the choice, which he saw as "meaningless and grossly inadequate," completely lacking in "heraldic and historical significance." Later he would labour diligently on the official Flag Proclamation. And eventually, according to his son, Charles, Beddoe would come to see the committee's compromise as an apt one.

Like so many old-stock Anglo Canadians of the 1960s, Alan Beddoe was initially far too close to the controversy to guess that the very absence of specific historical or heraldic references was part of the new flag's genius. It was indelibly an indigenous symbol for a new country, a country still finding itself. From this side of the turn of a new century, the Maple Leaf flag looks so obviously and unquestionably right that anyone born after the fact finds it almost impossible to fathom what all the fuss was about. There's no question, however, that the fuss was worth it.

New Zealanders and Australians who want a new flag have two powerful arguments in their favour. Their existing banners are both based on the British blue ensign, recalling their colonial past rather than autonomous present. And both flags have the constellation called the Southern Cross in the fly, making them easy to confuse. During a 1985 visit to Canada by the Australian prime minister, a New Zealand flag was mistakenly hoisted in his honour.

Recent Kiwi proposals tend to employ either the indigenous silver fern or the Southern Cross. The black-and-white stylized silver-fern flag (*top left*) is the work of Lloyd Morrison along with Cameron Sanders of the design firm Cato Partners. Jason Paul Troup's blue-white-and-green proposal (*bottom left*) combines the koru (a Maori symbol derived from a curled fern frond, which here also resembles a breaking wave) with the Southern Cross.

Australia's version of the Southern Cross (including a smaller fifth star) appears in many recent designs, including Mark Tucker's red-white-and-blue flag (*bottom right*), which won a 1993 competition prompted by the looming 2000 Sydney Olympics. The arc of red at the bottom represents an endless horizon. Far more daring is Harold Scruby's striking kangaroo flag (*top right*), featuring the red, black and yellow of the Aboriginal flag.

NEW ZEALAND

AUSTRALIA

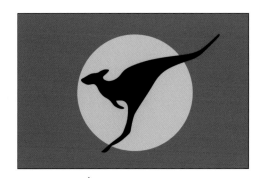

These four faces of Canada Day demonstrate how inextricably the Maple Leaf flag is woven into the Canadian fabric. (*Left to right*) Five-year-old Dezerae Aoudla; eight-year-old Kevin McHenry; fifteen-month-old Ivan Chen; twenty-month-old Cassandra Fode.

Pity our Australian and New Zealand cousins who are still wrestling to rid themselves of colonial symbols, still searching for truly indigenous flags to replace their versions of the blue British naval ensign. The Aussies have been at it since 1953, when Prime Minister Robert Menzies pushed a bill through parliament adopting the Australian Blue Ensign as the country's official national flag. (Legend has it that Menzies spurned the Red Ensign in previous use because he associated red with communism.) Through subsequent bursts of new-flag advocacy and several Australian flag contests, nothing close to a national consensus has emerged since. In New Zealand, one unofficial group has proposed a black flag emblazoned with a stylized silver fern, a native plant that appeared on soldiers' caps and collars in World War I and II, just as did our maple leaf. The website maintained by the fern flag's creators sounds a wistful note of flag envy: "Above all, we sought simplicity in the design of the fern, drawing on the efficacy of the simple design of such great flags as those of Switzerland, Japan and Canada."

A great flag, no question, simple and elegant in design, unmistakable even at a great distance, unique in its central symbol – a single, stylized red maple leaf. That symbolic leaf has come a long way since its humble start when some unnamed European colonist first adopted it as a homegrown emblem. It grew up fast in the years before Confederation but only earned its young adulthood on the battlefields of France and Belgium. After the country fought a second world war without a flag of its own, the maple leaf was finally ready to cut the last of its colonial apron strings and to take on its destined role. Since 1965, the flag has grown in stature and gained in meaning. In fewer than fifty years the Canadian Maple Leaf has come to set the standard for what a flag can be.

By the simple fact of being there, our flag has helped us grow into a country most people in the world would be proud to call their own. Today few would argue with historian Arthur Lower's words from 1967: "Since the adoption of the flag, something very interesting has happened to the Canadian psyche ... Each time that the average citizen looks at the new flag, he unconsciously says to himself, 'That's me!'"

"A flag may be defined as a piece of bunting or other pliable material which serves as a means of identification or as a signal. It is usually oblong or square in shape, attached at one end to a staff or halyard ... But a flag is more than a means of identification. It is the embodiment of what a country, province, church or regiment stands for: it is the symbol of the ethos or spirit of a people or community, its hopes, its aspirations, its will to live and its determination to play its role in history. A flag speaks for the people ... It silently calls all men and women to the service of the land in which they live. It inspires self-sacrifice, loyalty and devotion."

Historian GEORGE F.G. STANLEY, *The Story of Canada's Flag*, 1965

SOURCES

A comprehensive bibliography of books relevant to the story of the Canadian flag and its origins would fill many pages and include a host of privately published books and pamphlets, some espousing the retention of the Union Jack or the Red Ensign, others arguing for some new and distinctly Canadian banner. This list of books, articles and unpublished documents is confined to those that proved particularly useful in the writing of *A Flag for Canada* or that are quoted or cited in the text or captions.

The speech notes and memo written by John Diefenbaker from which I quote are in the Diefenbaker Centre Archives, Diefenbaker Centre, University of Saskatchewan.

Adams, Michael (with Amy Langstaff). *Unlikely Utopia: The Surprising Triumph of Canadian Pluralism.* Toronto: Viking Canada, 2007.

Baillargé, Frédéric Alexandre. *Le drapeau canadien-français : nos raisons* [pamphlet]. Montreal: Chez Granger, 1904.

Batten, Jack, ed. *Canada at the Olympics: The First Hundred Years, 1896-1996.* Toronto: INFACT Publishing, 1996.

Beddoe, Alan Brookman. Diaries, 1964. Private collection of Charles Beddoe.

———. Papers. National Archives of Canada, MG30, D252.

Berton, Pierre. *The Last Good Year: 1967.* Toronto: Doubleday Canada, 1997.

Biron, Luc André. *Le drapeau canadien.* Montreal: Les Éditions de l'Homme, 1962.

Bliss, Michael. "Privatizing the Mind: The Sundering of Canadian History, the Sundering of Canada." *Journal of Canadian Studies* 26, no. 4 (winter 1991).

Boswell, Randy. "The Simple Sketch That Created Our 'Unifying Symbol.'" *Ottawa Citizen*, February 15, 2002, pp A1, A4.

Brown, Craig, ed. *The Illustrated History of Canada.* Rev. ed. Toronto: Key Porter Books, 2000.

Canada. Department of the Secretary of State. *The National Flag of Canada / Le drapeau national du Canada.* Ottawa: Queen's Printer, 1966.

———. Parliament. House of Commons. *Debates.* 26th Parliament, 2nd Session, February 18, 1964, to April 3, 1965. Ottawa: Queen's Printer, 1965.

———. Parliament. Records. National Archives of Canada, RG 14, accession 87–88/146, boxes 101, 102, Special Committee on a Canadian Flag.

———. Privy Council Office. National Archives of Canada, RG2, accession 2000–01/376–7, boxes 171, 172.

———. Secretary of State. National Archives of Canada, RG6, vols. 459-89, Records of the Special Committee on the Canadian Flag.

Carnochan, Janet. "The Origin of the Maple Leaf as the Emblem of Canada." *Papers and Records.* Ontario Historical Society. Vol. 7 (1906): 139-46.

The Charlton Standard Catalogue of Canadian Coins. 56th ed. Toronto: Charlton Press, 2002.

The Charlton Standard Catalogue of First World War Canadian Badges. 1st ed. Toronto: Charlton Press, 1995.

Cinemedia Presents the Canadian Flag [film]. Directed by Ann Pearson, produced by Joseph Koenig, script by Howard Greenspan. Toronto: Cinemedia, 1973.

Cobb, David. "Our Great Flag Mystery." *Canadian Magazine.* January 26, 1974.

Cook, Ramsay. *Canada, Quebec, and the Uses of Nationalism.* 2nd edition. Toronto: McClelland & Stewart, 1995.

Côté, Ephrem. *Project of a Distinct National Flag for Canada/Projet du drapeau national distinct pour le Canada* [booklet]. Privately published, 1939.

Creighton, Donald, et al. "Canada's National Symbols: An Appeal to Mr. Pearson." *The Canadian Forum*, June 1964, p 54.

Diefenbaker, John G. *One Canada: Memoirs of the Right Honourable John G. Diefenbaker.* Vol. 3, *The Tumultuous Years, 1962–1967.* Toronto: Macmillan of Canada, 1977.

———. Papers. National Archives of Canada, MG26, M.

Duffy, John. *Fights of Our Lives: Elections, Leadership and the Making of Canada.* Toronto: HarperCollins, 2002.

English, John. *Shadow of Heaven: 1897–1948.* Vol. 1 of *The Life of Lester Pearson.* Toronto: Lester & Orpen Dennys, 1989.

———. *The Worldly Years: 1949–1972.* Vol. 2 of *The Life of Lester Pearson.* Toronto: Knopf Canada, 1992.

Ewart, John S. *Sir John A. Macdonald and the Canadian Flag* [pamphlet]. Ottawa: privately published, [1907].

Fleming, Sandford. "The Canadian Flag: Proposal for the Meteor Flag of the Dominion." *The Week*, May 31, 1895, front and back cover, p 639.

Fraser, Alistair. "A Canadian Flag for Canada." *Journal of Canadian Studies* 25 (4): 64–80.

Fraser, Blair. *The Search for Identity: Canada, 1945–1967.* Canadian History Series. Toronto: Doubleday Canada, 1967.

Gale, Jack. "What Canadians Want in a Flag." *Star Weekly*, March 21, 1959.

Granatstein, J.L. *Canada 1957–1967: The Years of Uncertainty and Innovation.* Canadian Centenary Series. Toronto: McClelland & Stewart, 1986.

Greaves, Kevin. *A Canadian Heraldic Primer.* Ottawa: Heraldry Society of Canada, 2000.

Gwyn, Richard. *Nationalism Without Walls: The Unbearable Lightness of Being Canadian.* Toronto: McClelland & Stewart, 1995.

Hehner, Barbara, ed. *The Spirit of Canada.* Toronto: Malcolm Lester Books, 1999.

Holt, Simma. *The Other Mrs. Diefenbaker.* Toronto: Doubleday Canada, 1982.

Hosie, R.C. *Native Trees of Canada.* Toronto: Fitzhenry & Whiteside, 1979.

Hutcheon, Linda. "As Canadian as Possible . . . Under the Circumstances!" In *The Canadian Essay*, edited by Gerald Lynch and David Rampton. Toronto: Copp Clark Pitman, 1991.

Ibbitson, John. *Loyal No More: Ontario's Struggle for a Separate Destiny.* Toronto: HarperCollins, 2001.

———. *The Polite Revolution: Perfecting the Canadian Dream.* Toronto: McClelland & Stewart, 2005.

"In Search of a Meaningful Canadian Symbolism." *Canadian Art*, September/October 1963, pp 272–75.

Inauguration of the National Flag of Canada/Inauguration du drapeau national du Canada [film]. Montreal: National Film Board of Canada, 1965.

Kaplan, William, ed. *Belonging: The Meaning and Future of Canadian Citizenship* Montreal and Kingston: McGill-Queen's University Press, 1993.

Kearney, Richard. *On Stories.* London and New York: Routledge, 2002.

Kent, Tom. *A Public Purpose: An Experience of Liberal Opposition and Canadian Government.* Kingston and Montreal: McGill-Queen's University Press, 1988.

Kerr, Wilfred Brenton. *Arms and the Maple Leaf: Memories of Canada's Corps, 1918.* Seaforth, Ont.: Huron Expositor Press, 1943.

Liberal Party of Canada. Papers. National Archives of Canada, MG28, IV, 3.

Ligue du drapeau national. *For a National Flag/Pour un drapeau national* [pamphlet]. Quebec: Ligue du drapeau national, [1943].

Lind, Jane. *Joyce Wieland: Artist on Fire.* Toronto: James Lorimer & Company, 2001.

Lower, Arthur. "Centennial Ends: Centennial Begins." *Queen's Quarterly* 74, no. 2 (summer 1967): 236–41.

Lynch, Gerald, and David Rampton, eds. *The Canadian Essay.* Toronto: Copp Clark Pitman, 1991.

MacGregor, Roy. *Canadians: A Portrait of a Country and Its People.* Toronto: Viking Canada, 2007.

Matheson, John Ross. *Canada's Flag: A Search for a Country.* Belleville, Ontario: Mika, 1986.

———. Papers. National Archives of Canada, MG30, C29.

McKeown, Robert. "How Canada's Flag Was Born." *Weekend Magazine*, January 23, 1965, pp 13–14, 30.

Moncreiffe, Iain, and Don Pottinger. *Simple Heraldry.* London: Thomas Nelson and Sons, 1956.

Monteith, Jay Waldo. Diary of the 1964 Flag Committee. Monteith Papers, National Archives of Canada. MG32, B29.

Morris, J.H. "The Origin of Our Maple Leaf Emblem." *Papers and Records.* Ontario Historical Society. Vol. 5 (1904): 21–35.

The National Flag of Canada: A Profile. Ottawa: Department of Canadian Heritage, Canadian Identity Directorate, 2000.

Newman, Peter C. *The Distemper of Our Times: Canadian Politics in Transition, 1963–1968.* Toronto: McClelland & Stewart, 1968.

News in Review, May 1998 [videocassette and resource guide]. Toronto: Canadian Broadcasting Corporation, 1998.

Nicholson, Patrick. *Vision and Indecision.* Toronto: Longmans Canada, 1968.

North, Susan. "The Great Debate." *The Archivist* (January- February 1990): 14–15.

Owens, Ann-Maureen, and Jane Yealland. *Canada's Maple Leaf: The Story of Our Flag.* Toronto and Buffalo: Kids Can Press, 1999.

Pearson, Lester B. *Mike: The Memoirs of the Rt. Hon. Lester B. Pearson*, vol. 3. Toronto: University of Toronto Press, 1977.

———. Papers. National Archives of Canada, MG26 N.

———. *Words and Occasions: An Anthology of Speeches and Articles.* Toronto: University of Toronto Press, 1970.

Podnieks, Andrew. *Hockey's Greatest Teams: Teams, Players, and Plays That Changed the Game.* Toronto: Penguin, 2000.

Progressive Conservative Party of Canada. Papers. National Archives of Canada, MG28, IV, 2.

Reid, Patrick. *Wild Colonial Boy: A Memoir.* Vancouver: Douglas & McIntyre, 1995.

Richler, Mordecai. *Home Sweet Home: My Canadian Album.* Toronto: McClelland & Stewart, 1984.

Richler, Noah. *This Is My Country, What's Yours? A Literary Atlas of Canada.* Toronto: McClelland & Stewart, 2006.

Smith, Denis. *Rogue Tory: The Life and Legend of John G. Diefenbaker.* Toronto: Macfarlane Walter & Ross, 1995.

Stanley, George F.G. *The Story of Canada's Flag: A Historical Sketch.* Toronto: Ryerson Press, 1965.

Stewart, Walter. "The Great Flag Fight." *Star Weekly*, July 4, 1964.

Stursberg, Peter. *Lester Pearson and the Dream of Unity.* Toronto: Doubleday Canada, 1978.

Swan, Conrad. *Canada: Symbols of Sovereignty.* Toronto and Buffalo: University of Toronto Press, 1977.

Trudeau, Pierre Elliott. *Memoirs.* Toronto: McClelland & Stewart, 1993.

Way, Alan. "The Government of Canada's Federal Identity Program." *Design Management Journal* 4, no. 3 (summer 1993): 54–62.

Whalen, James M. "Canada's Flag: Minority Designs Unfurled." *The Archivist* (January-February 1990): 18–20.

Woodcock, Thomas, and John Martin Robinson. *The Oxford Guide to Heraldry.* Oxford: Oxford University Press, 1988.

Wozniak, Maurice D., ed. *Krause-Minkus Standard Catalog of Canadian & United Nations Stamps.* Iola, Wisc.: Krause Publications, 1999.

Wright, Glenn. *"First" Flags: A Report on Research Undertaken to Identify and Locate Canada's First Maple Leaf Flags* [PDF file]. National Archives of Canada, 2001. <www.archives.ca/04/0430/0430_e.html>

Zeman, Ludmila. *The First Red Maple Leaf.* Toronto: Tundra Books, 1997.

Znamierowski, Alfred. *The World Encyclopedia of Flags: The Definitive Guide to International Flags, Banners, Standards and Ensigns.* London: Hermes House, 1999, 2001.

FRONT MATTER

p v: Bruce Law/Russell Porter Collection; p vi: Ted Grant/CMCP 64-3976.

CHAPTER ONE

p 2: PAM; p 4: Duncan Macpherson, reprinted with permission – The Toronto Star Syndicate; p 5: Bruce Law/109 Branch RCL; p 8: LAC PA-107910; p 9: left: LAC C-131328; middle: C-029568; right: CWM AN-19780473-030; pp 10–11: Carl Vincent; p 13: Montreal Gazette Archives; pp 14–15: AGO; pp 16–17: Department of Canadian Heritage, Website, reproduced with the permission of the Minister of Public Works and Government Services of Canada; p 18: copyright Canada Post Corporation, 1964, reproduced with permission; p 19: Norman James/Toronto Star; p 20: CP; p 21: left: courtesy of Charles Beddoe; bottom right: courtesy of Charles Beddoe, photographer unknown; pp 22–23: Ted Grant/CMCP 64-3992; p 25: Montreal Star Collection/LAC PA-213156; p 27: CP; p 28: left: LAC/Duncan Cameron PA-136779; right: Montreal Star Collection/LAC PA-213162.

CHAPTER TWO

p 30: courtesy of the Canadian Forces; p 32–33: Kent Kallberg/Russell Porter Collection; p 35: top left: NA-667-145, top right: NA-667-148; bottom: Keystone View Co./LAC PA-207560; p 36: Dean Kujala/Joseph Iorio Collection; p 39: left: LAC NL-13466; right: Milton Adamson/LAC PA-030217; p 40: Vancouver Maritime Museum; p 41: Kent Kallberg; p 43: copyright Canada Post Corporation, 1851, reproduced with permission; p 44: courtesy of TFRBL, University of Toronto; p 45: LAC C-006536; p 46: courtesy of TFRBL, University of Toronto; p 47: from the collection of Chateau Ramezay, Montreal, 1998-1619; p 48: courtesy of TFRBL, University of Toronto; p 49: Royal Canadian Regiment Museum; p 50: left, centre left, centre right: CWM; right, bottom, Bruce Law/109 Branch, RCL; p 51: left, centre right: CWM; centre left, right: Bruce Law/109 Branch, RCL; p 52: DND/LAC PA-003667; p 53: DND/LAC PA-002888; pp 54–55: Pringle & Booth/LAC PA-060562; p 55: PAM Canadian Army Photo 162 N10857; p 56: LAC PA-131395; p 57: top: Carl Vincent Collection; bottom: courtesy of the Canadian Forces; p 58: F.R. Halliday/Canadian National Exhibition Archives; p 59: courtesy of TFRBL, University of Toronto; p 60: LAC PA-150994; p 61: left: Charles A. Aylett/LAC C-014090; centre and right: CSHF; p 62–63, courtesy of the Canadian Heraldic Authority/Rd. Rev. D. Ralph Spence collection/Ray Peterson, Photo Features; p 64: LAC PA-212141; p 65: Bruce Law; p 66: courtesy of Maclean's Magazine.

CHAPTER THREE

p 68: Duncan Cameron/LAC PA-142624; p 70: Dean Kujala; p 71: Duncan Cameron/LAC PA-136148; p 72: Duncan Cameron/LAC PA-139887; p 73: John Collins/Toronto Telegram; pp 74–75: courtesy of QUA John Matheson fonds, locator V016; p 77: top: Duncan Cameron/LAC PA-136154; p 78: left, top to bottom: LAC 1979-75-72; LAC 1979-75-33; LAC 1979-75-64; right, top to bottom: LAC 1979-75-107; LAC 1979-75-85; LAC 1979-75-60; LAC 1979-75-88; p 79: left, top to bottom: LAC 1979-75-86; LAC 1979-75-35; LAC 1979-75-97-1; LAC 1979-75-93; centre, top to bottom: LAC 1979-75-26; LAC 1979-75-94; LAC 1979-75-76; LAC 1979-75-73; right, top to bottom: LAC 1979-75-40; LAC 1979-75-84; LAC 1979-75-97-2; LAC 1979-75-75; p 82: LAC C-149330; p 83: left, top to bottom: LAC C-149323; LAC C-149324; LAC C-149329; LAC C-149325; centre, top to bottom: LAC C-149322; LAC C-149320; LAC C-149321; LAC C-149327; right, top to bottom: LAC C-149326; LAC C-149319; LAC C-149328; pp 84–85: Eddy Rowarth/The Toronto Star; p 86: CP; p 87: CP; p 88: Dean Kujala; p 89: Andy Donato/Toronto Telegram; p 90: Darrel Kennedy; p 91: Royal Military College; p 92: George Stanley; p 95: LAC C-149463; p 96: LAC C-149464; p 97: LAC C-149462; p 99: Dean Kujala; p 102: Kent Kallberg/Russell Porter Collection; p 103: courtesy of QUA John Matheson fonds, locator BT FOLIO B-1; p 105: Bruce Law; p 106: LAC C-135374; p 110: Kent Kallberg.

CHAPTER FOUR

p 112: Brian Willer; p 114: left: LAC PA-149878; right: courtesy of the Canadian Forces; p 115: Dick Darell/The Toronto Star; p 116: CP/WFP; p 119: CMCP 65-625; p 120: left: Canadian National Exhibiton Foundation; p 121: Brian Willer; pp 122–123: I-51545, supplied by BC Archives; p 124: Dean Kujala; p 125: left: CMC, 77-1045/S85-4366; right: CMC, 77-1045/S89-1509; p 126: Dean Kujala; p 127: Dean Kujala; p 128: Diefenbaker Centre for the Study of Canada, University of Saskatchewan; p 129: Duncan Cameron/LAC PA-111213; pp 130 131: LAC C-30085; p 131: Dean Kujala/Joseph Iorio Collection; p 133: courtesy of the Canadian Forces; p 134: copyright Pierre St. Jacques/Imagination Photo Services; p 135: top: Dean Kujala; bottom: CBC Still Photo Collection; p 136: NGC; p 137: left: Charles Pachter; right: AGO/copyright Estate Christiane Pflug; p 138: Air Canada Corporate Records/Archives; p 139: the Arms of Canada, the flag symbol, and the "Canada" wordmark are protected as official marks of the Government of Canada under the Trade-Marks Act, and are reproduced with the permission of the Government of Canada; p 140: Roberto Dosil; p 141: 1: courtesy of the Canadian Snowboard Federation; 2: courtesy of the Canadian Grain Commission; 3: courtesy of the Toronto Blue Jays Baseball Club; 4: courtesy of the Canadian Museum of Civilization; p 142: 1: courtesy of Air Canada; 2: courtesy of Canadian Tire Corporation; 3: Marque de commerce de Petro-Canada – Trademark; 4: courtesy of Hockey Hall of Fame; 5: Canada Science and Technology Museum/CN Collection; p 143: Roberto Dosil/Greyhound Lines Ltd; the Greyhound running dog and name are registered trademarks of Greyhound Lines, Inc. and used by permission; p 144: CP/Peter Bregg

CHAPTER FIVE

p 148: Roberto Dosil; p 150: CP/Toronto Star; p 151: IWM 005361/Crown copyright; p 152: top: c P/Hans Deryk; bottom: c P/Fred Chartrand; p 153: reproduced with the permission of Veterans Affairs Canada; p 154: c P/Jonathan Hayward; p 155: c P/Fred Chartrand; p 156: Kent Kallberg; p 157: top left: courtesy of the Canadian Forces, MCpl Ken Allan; top right: courtesy of the Canadian Forces; bottom: courtesy of the Canadian Forces, Lt Laura Oberwarth; p 158: courtesy of the Chancellery of Honours, Office of the Secretary to the Governor General, Government of Canada; p 159: c P/Jonathan Hayward; p 160–161: c P/ Andrew Vaughan; p 162: c P/Tom Hanson; p 163: left: c P/Paul Chiasson; right: c P/Andrew Vaughan; p 164: Canadian Space Agency; p 165: Ian Smith/Vancouver Sun; p 166: c P/Rusty Kennedy; p 166–167: c P/AP/Lawrence Jackson; p 168: c P/Tom Hanson; p 169: courtesy of the Canadian Forces, Sgt Dennis Mah; p 171: reproduced by permission of the Canadian Tourism Commission; p 172: c P/Tom Hanson; p 173: c P/Tom Hanson; p 174: courtesy of the Canadian Heraldic Authority; p 175: top left: Cameron Sanders, bottom left: Jason Paul Troup, top right: Harold Scruby, bottom right: Mark Tucker; p 176: left to right: c P/John Hasyn; c P/Toronto Star/Ron Bull; c P/Edmonton Sun/ Darryl Dyck; c P/Medicine Hat News/ Deddeda Stemmler.

The author wishes to thank the following copyright holders for permission to quote or reproduce their materials.

Charles Beddoe: excerpts from Alan Brookman Beddoe diary for October and December 1964.

Robert McKeown, Jr.: excerpt from *Weekend Magazine* article, January 23, 1965, by his father, Robert McKeown.

George F.G. Stanley: letter to John Matheson, March 23, 1964.

Warner Bros. Publications U.S. Inc., Miami, Florida 33014: excerpt from Freddy Grant, *The Flag of Canada*, © 1965 Gordon V. Thompson Music (Socan), copyright renewed, all rights reserved, used by permission.

Sally Wismer: excerpts from the 1964 Flag Committee diary of her father, Jay Waldo Monteith, and his sketches of the group C flag designs.

ACKNOWLEDGMENTS

For the first edition
Like the maple leaf flag, this book, has had many authors. Chief among these collaborators has been Roberto Dosil, the book's designer, who was also the project's prime mover. His stunning design eloquently communicates the way he feels about his adopted country and his editorial imprint is on every page. This book is as much his as mine.

Many others made important contributions, above all John Matheson, who gave his time in several interviews, lent me portions of his unpublished book on the Order of Canada and helped in any way he could. Other participants in the events of 1964–65 who agreed to be interviewed were Joseph Macaluso, Patrick Reid and Reid Scott.

Carl and Elizabeth Vincent mined the holdings of Library and Archives Canada for the original documents and images that help set this book apart. Perhaps their greatest find was the diary kept by Jay Waldo Monteith, the Conservative point man on the 1964 Flag Committee. Monteith's private musings provided a fresh angle on a part of the story that has tended to petrify into myth.

Several others read and commented on the text, either in whole or in part: Bruce Cane, Paul Delaney, Roberto Dosil, Jim Douglas, Ward McBurney, Christopher Moore, Allen Seager, Mark Stanton and Morris Wolfe. The errors that remain, of course, are mine.

Of the many people who helped shape the text and visuals, one stands out. Ward McBurney guided my visit to Alexander Muir's maple tree, made the connection between the laurel wreath of antiquity and the First World War maple leaf wreath of vic-tory and fed me countless morsels of information, perception and encouragement.

But there are so many others. Charles Beddoe transcribed portions of his father's 1964 diary and opened his personal archive of memory and memorabilia. Carolyn Bennett, MP, and her executive assistant, Robert White, arranged for me to visit Committee Room 356S, where the Flag Committee deliberated. Randy Boswell of the *Ottawa Citizen* blazed the trail to Charles Beddoe and Reid Scott. Donna Braggins and her *Maclean's* colleagues Fernanda Pisani, Joe Power and Hazel Willis produced a scan of Rex Woods's 1954 *Maclean's* flag cover in record time. Bill Bruce used his Stratford network to help me contact Waldo Monteith's heirs. Bruce Cane tracked down the photograph of the Royal Canadian Regiment at Paardeberg in 1899. Heather Ebbs recommended both the best researchers and the best photographer in Ottawa. Susan Haines scrolled through hours of videos of the 1992 World Series. Anna Hudson of the Art Gallery of Ontario pointed out examples of the flag as a motif in Canadian art. Grant Johnson provided details of the Federal Identity Program. Bill Kretzler explained the evolution of government design in the 1960s. Elizabeth Matte of the Canadian Association of Former Parliamentarians tracked down living members of the Flag Committee. Ian Miller discovered Isabel Graham's poem "The Maple Leaves." Kathy Murphy, constituency assistant to John Richardson, MP for Perth, aided the search for Waldo Monteith's daughters. The people at Otherwise Editions lent photos from their archive. Rob Paul of the Diefenbaker Centre Archives ensured that my brief visit to Saskatoon would be extraordinarily productive. Ken

Polsson pointed me to useful information on the history of Canadian coins. Allen Seager explained how the story of the maple leaf emblem typified the appropriation of French-Canadian symbols by English Canada. Jamie Serran at Macfarlane Walter & Ross chased down information and checked facts.

Thanks also to: Susan Barrable; Nathan Beyerle; Joy Cohnstaedt; Charles Ebbs; Jackie Martin; Duncan Matheson; Christine Mosser of the Baldwin Collection, Toronto Reference Library; Sharon Shipley of Library and Archives Canada; Wendy Watts of Toronto Star Photo Services; the staff of the Thomas Fisher Rare Book Library, University of Toronto; Sally Monteith Wismer.

Special thanks to the people who edited, produced and published the first edition of this book. Don Atkins, Mark Stanton and Roberto Dosil of Stanton Atkins & Dosil Productions packaged the idea and produced the magnificent end product. Brian Scrivener provided solid editorial support. Eva Veres cleared a dizzying number of permissions. Stephanie Fysh prepared the fine index. Jan Walter of Macfarlane Walter & Ross not only launched me on my flag odyssey but gave the book that resulted its first home. She and her colleague Barbara Czarnecki saw to it that as little as possible slipped through the cracks created by intense deadline pressure and long lines of communication. MW&R Associate Editor Adrienne Guthrie provided superb administrative support.

For the second edition
This second edition has been immeasurably enriched by the help and advice of the following: Charles Beddoe; Greg Cable and his father Howard, the seemingly immortal Canadian conductor and composer; Canadian War Museum (George Barnhill, Tim Cook, John Corneil, Eric Fernberg, Shelley Stairs); Linda Cobon, Records and Archives, Canadian National Exhibition; Imperial War Museum, London (Richard Bayford, Martin Boswell, Katie Jude, Yvonne Oliver, Roger Tolson, Fernanda Torrente, Rosalind Whitford); Paul "Smokie" LeBlanc, Senior Ceremonial Officer, Canadian Symbols, Canadian Heritage; Library and Archives Canada (Martha Catchpole, Mary Margaret Johnston-Miller); David Morrison, Canadian Museum of Civilization; Kerry Pither; Bill Reddick; Linda Roberts, Statistics Canada; Janice Summerby, Veterans Affairs; Royal Canadian Legion (Bob Butt, Duane Daly, Anne Reid, Brad White); Bishop Ralph Spence; Athina Tagidou; Glenn Wright.

Particular words of thanks go to two individuals. Darrel Kennedy, Assiniboine Herald, the Canadian Heraldic Authority, corrected heraldic bloopers from the first edition, connected us with the extraordinary flag collection of Bishop Ralph Spence (which made possible the new feature on the history of the Canadian Red Ensign), helped me track down the now-retired Glenn Wright, and vetted several sections of text. Mary Margaret Johnston-Miller of Library and Archives Canada pursued the hunt for the missing flag finalists (twelve of fifteen) far beyond the call of her job description. She hasn't yet tracked down all the culprits, but if anyone can, she will.

Barbara Tomlin provided substantive editing of the highest order, while also being a pleasure to work with. Ruth Wilson skillfully copy edited and proofed the new material and caught a few embarrassing glitches in the original edition.

Finally and as always, thanks to Rick Feldman.

Rick Archbold

To Harriet and Bill, who taught me
the meaning of citizenship

R.A.

To Canada

R.D.

LIBRARY AND ARCHIVES CANADA CATALOGUING IN PUBLICATION

Archbold, Rick, 1950–
    A flag for Canada / Rick Archbold.

First published under title: I stand for Canada.
Includes bibliographical references and index.
ISBN 978-0-9732346-9-5 / paperback
ISBN 978-0-9732346-8-8 / bound

1. Flags – Canada – History.
2. Maple leaf (Emblem).
3. Canada – History – 1963.
4. Canada – Politics and government – 1963–1968.
I. Title.

CR115.C2A72 2008   929.9'20971   C2008-903000-1

Stanton Atkins & Dosil Publishers
Mailing address
2632 Bronte Drive
North Vancouver, BC
Canada, V7H 1M4

Edited by: Barbara Tomlin
Proofread by: Ruth Wilson
Indexed by: Naomi Pauls
Designed by: Roberto Dosil
Colour preparation by: Ernst Vegt
Printed and bound by: C&C Offset, China

This book's titles, text, sidebars, and
captions are typeset in Cartier, a type-
face family originally designed by
Carl Dair between 1957 and 1967. Rod
McDonald redesigned and expanded
the family between 1998 and 2000.
The stock is 157gms Japanese Newage
Blanc FSC matte art, produced by
Oji Paper at their Tomioka mill.

SECOND EDITION / FIRST PRINTING